The Kingdom of God Changes Everything

Buck Black

Cover design: Katie Martin
Cover image: Ralph Ravi Kayden / Unsplash

Ebook: ISBN 978-1-7367588-0-9
Paperback: ISBN: 978-1-7367588-1-6

DEDICATION

This book is dedicated to my beloved family—Pegi, Eli, Anita, Titus, Felicity, Mike, Kati, Connie, Gwen, Jackie, Peter, and Kaitlin. You were all with me throughout this long writing process. My prayer is that each of you would come to be gripped by this great truth proclaimed by Jesus Himself that the Kingdom of God truly is the great treasure—the "pearl of great value"—in this life and the life to come, worth selling everything else for. May it surprise you as it has surprised me. Oh that I might see each of you again in heaven.

CONTENTS

1

It's All About the Kingdom

SOMETIMES, YOUR LIFE CAN CHANGE with a simple question.

"Do you love me?"

"Is it cancer?"

"Will you forgive me?"

"Do you want fries with that?" (OK, maybe not that question.)

THE BIG QUESTION IN THIS BOOK

As life altering as the above questions can be (except fries), every person faces another question that is more profound and eternally significant. Every person faces it because God Himself asks it. Even a non-answer is an answer. Answer it wrong to your eternal peril. But, if answered correctly, it will change your life dramatically both here on Earth and eternally.

It is a two-part question: *What is the Kingdom of God and why does it matter?*

We answer the question in subsequent chapters. However, it is vital to first understand why the question is so important. If scripture doesn't treat it as the first order of importance, then why should we? As it turns out, Jesus Himself speaks passionately and at length about the Kingdom. So before we consider what the Kingdom of God[1] is, let's consider its place of importance in the scriptures, particularly from Jesus Himself. Once we realize its centrality to the whole of scripture, we can then begin to answer the question.

JESUS' PURPOSE

Why did Jesus come to earth? Why did He leave heaven, take on human flesh, die on the cross, and ascend to heaven? What was the purpose? Before you answer, listen to Jesus's own answer: Luke 4:43 says, "I must preach the good news of the *kingdom of God* to the other towns as well; *for I was sent for this purpose*" (emphasis added).

Stop and let that sink in. Jesus certainly came to seek and to save those who were lost (Luke 19:10) But why did he do so? The fundamental reason Jesus came was to declare the good news that the Kingdom of God was being established, and he set about making it a reality through His incarnation, life, death, and resurrection.

Some may want to infer that the "good news of the Kingdom" was the gospel as we think of it, the gospel of salvation. But that isn't supported by Jesus's preaching during His three year ministry. Nowhere in the Gospels do we read of Jesus proclaiming here on Earth that we must repent of our sins and believe in His life and death as the basis for our justification and adoption as God's children.[2] Instead, throughout the gospels, Jesus teaches about and expounds on

---

1) For purposes of this book, the terms "Kingdom of God" and "Kingdom of Heaven" are considered to be the same. Some theologians treat the two as related but separate. However, this book accepts the explanation that Kingdom of Heaven was used by Matthew for Jewish believers.
2) In Mark 8: 31-33, Jesus tells His disciples that He must be killed and rise again in three days. But this is said only to His disciples. In John 3: 13-15, Jesus says that He must be lifted up and whoever believes in Him will be have eternal life. In both instances, he does not explain what this accomplishes or how to receive it. The gospel of salvation as we know it isn't explicitly taught in the Gospels; it is proclaimed subsequent to His death and resurrection.

the Kingdom of God. The good news in Luke 4:43 is the Kingdom of God, not the gospel of salvation.

Everything else proceeds from this good news of the Kingdom of God—the gospel of salvation, the church, His teachings such as the Sermon on the Mount, and all of the epistles. They all are subsumed under this reason why Jesus came. The Kingdom was the prime reason Jesus came. And that's big.

SEEK IT FIRST

Matthew 6:33 says, "But *seek first the kingdom of God* and his righteousness, and all these things will be added to you" (emphasis added).

Wait. What?

How many times have I read this passage and not stopped to consider what it is really saying? When I have considered it, in my rush I've thought this passage was saying seek Jesus first. Or seek salvation first.

Wrong.

Of all the things we are to seek out in this life, the first, the pre-eminent, is the Kingdom of God. Nothing is more important to Jesus than our finding, entering, and living in the Kingdom of God. Nothing.

Let's be honest with ourselves. What do we seek most in life? In my life, the answer varied at different times: it was pursuing my wife to be my wife. It was success in my job. It was financial prosperity. It was raising my children to become believers. Jesus says, "That's not what you should seek first…" I missed the whole point.

What do you think the first thing is that you should seek? Should we seek racial justice first? Or perhaps, we should seek solutions to climate change. We worry that human existence is threatened. Or fight to end abortion. Shouldn't we first and foremost end the death of the unborn? These are vital issues for sure.

At a more personal level, you probably are going to say, "to be saved." Or you didn't want to go to hell. Or you should seek Jesus—a savior, a friend, a brother.

To all of this, Jesus is saying, "Not good enough. Seek first the Kingdom of God."

Notice the promise in the above scripture: if we seek the Kingdom first "all these things will be added to you." What things will be added? Specifically in the immediate passage Jesus says that food and clothing will be added to us. But more broadly, if we reread the entire Sermon on the Mount, He is saying that everything we seek—justice, righteousness, peace, community, even salvation itself—come with the Kingdom.

But first? It's the Kingdom of God.

INESTIMABLE VALUE

Jesus tells us about the incomparable worth of the Kingdom of God relative to everything else:

> The kingdom of heaven is like treasure hidden in a field, which a man found and covered up. Then in his joy he goes and sells all that he has and buys that field. Again, the kingdom of heaven is like a merchant in search of fine pearls, who, on finding one pearl of great value, went and sold all that he had and bought it (Matthew 13: 44-45).

Jesus does not say add it to our portfolio of heart treasures: family, friends, job, marriage, children, home, money, status. It is so valuable, a person who rightly knows its worth *will willingly and joyfully sell everything to gain it.*

Most financial advisors will tell you that owning too much of one particular stock is too risky. If its value drops, your overall finances will be hit too hard and your standard of living will be adversely affected. The wise move is to sell some of it and invest it in other stocks to reduce the risk. It's called rebalancing.

Jesus doesn't want us to rebalance the Kingdom of God with our other treasures. He says sell it *all* for the Kingdom of Heaven. Everything you have that you think is valuable doesn't compare to the Kingdom of God. It means that you no longer put any fundamental/existential value in anything other than the Kingdom. Spare nothing in order to gain it.

Of course it is good to have family. It is good to prepare for your retirement. But their value comes only as they come back to you once you have gained the Kingdom and only if losing them wouldn't mean the end of your world, physically, emotionally, spiritually. We can lose everything else, as incredibly hard as that may be in some cases, but we can't afford to lose the Kingdom. Easy to say, of course. It's only possible as the Holy Spirit helps us understand how truly wonderful the Kingdom of God is that we can make that exchange in our hearts.

THE EVERLASTING KINGDOM

The Kingdom of God should be foremost in our minds because it is an everlasting kingdom. And Jesus is the King of that eternal kingdom. Peter calls it "the eternal kingdom of our Lord and Savior Jesus Christ" (2 Peter 1:11).

Think of it this way: At some point in history, no one else will be saved. There will be no need for repentance. No one else will be born again. But the Kingdom will be there. A million years from now. A billion years. A trillion years. It is an everlasting kingdom.

While the gospel shows us the way to salvation and bestows priceless gifts, someday there will be no more proclamation of the gospel; however, the reign and rule of the King in His Kingdom will be forever.

Consider then how much we should value the Kingdom of God now in light of how much we value an eternity with Jesus. For the Kingdom is our present AND our future. Russell Moore illuminates this idea thusly:

> A skewed vision of the future has consequences, both person-ally and socially. I often cringe when I hear Christians talk about the lists of things they want to do before they die. "I really want to go sky-diving, at least once before I die" or "I want to, just one time, climb Mount Kilimanjaro before I am too old to do it" or "I want to see the pyramids, before I'm gone." … If we assume that what's waiting for us beyond the grave is a postlude rather than a mission and an adventure, we will cling tenaciously to the status quo, or at least the parts of it we like.[3]

If we think the best of life is now, we've failed to grasp Jesus's passion. Failed. If we think the best of our life is rooted here in this life, we've missed the entire point of our salvation.

PASSED ONTO AND PROCLAIMED BY THE DISCIPLES

Nor should we think that the Kingdom of God was taught by Jesus only in the Gospels.

We know that upon His resurrection, Jesus appears to the disciples and lives among them for forty days before ascending. It must have been such an amazing time. Imagine living with the risen

3 Russell Moore, *Onward* (B&H Books, 2015) p 52

Savior! Eating with Him. Drinking with Him. Sitting beside Him. Walking with Him. Talking to Him. Listening to the risen Jesus.

And then we read this arresting passage in Act 1:3: "He presented himself alive to them after his suffering by many proofs, appearing to them during forty days and *speaking about the kingdom of God*" (emphasis added).

Of all that Jesus talks about during those forty days, the one thing that is called out specifically in scripture is the "Kingdom of God". Surely He spoke about the meaning and import of His death and resurrection in salvation. But Luke records that it was the Kingdom—Jesus's passion and purpose—which He spoke about in particular.

Jesus started His ministry calling the Kingdom of God His purpose for coming. He closes His time on earth giving the apostles a crash course on the Kingdom of God. The Kingdom of God is the bookends of His teaching. He passes it on to them.

Furthermore, what is that they ask Him before he ascends? In Acts 1:6, we read: "So when they had come together, they asked him, 'Lord, will you at this time restore *the kingdom* to Israel?'" (emphasis added).

The Kingdom of God is still uppermost in the apostles' minds throughout the early church age. How do we know this? Throughout the book of Acts, we read how the disciples proclaimed the Kingdom when preaching the gospel:

Philip in Samaria—"But when they believed Philip as *he preached good news about the kingdom of God* and the name of Jesus Christ, they were baptized, both men and women" (Acts 8:12, emphasis added).

Paul in Corinth—"And he entered the synagogue and for three months spoke boldly, reasoning and *persuading them about the kingdom of God*" (Acts 19: 8, emphasis added).

Paul in Rome—"He lived there two whole years at his own expense, and welcomed all who came to him, *proclaiming the kingdom of God* and teaching about the Lord Jesus Christ with all boldness and without hindrance" (Acts 28: 31-32, emphasis added).

Do you see it? The Kingdom of God was part of the gospel presentation. Faith in Jesus AND the Kingdom of God were both part of the apostolic proclamation of the gospel. It wasn't just a message of repentance and faith. The good news was that salvation is found in Jesus Christ and that we also enter into the glorious, eternal Kingdom of God in this life.

Likewise, we read of the Kingdom in the epistles:

I Corinthians 4:20 says: "For *the kingdom of God* does not consist in talk but in power" (emphasis added).

Hebrews 12:28 says: "Therefore let us be grateful *for receiving a kingdom* that cannot be shaken, and thus let us offer to God acceptable worship, with reverence and awe" (emphasis added).

So we see that the Kingdom of God is actually a centerpiece throughout the New Testament. It was Jesus's passion and purpose. It was proclaimed along with the gospel of salvation. It is the center from which our power emerges. We are called to be grateful for receiving it. It is part of the basis for our worship. The Kingdom of God is meant to be vibrantly alive in our hearts and minds and behavior.

UNDERSTAND THE KINGDOM OF GOD, UNDERSTAND JESUS

Understanding that the Kingdom was Jesus's purpose and passion and that it was part of the apostolic proclamation of the gospel means that failure to understand the Kingdom of God is a failure to understand Jesus. Consider this quote from Gordon Fee:

> You cannot know anything about Jesus, anything… if you miss the Kingdom of God. You are zero on Jesus if you don't understand the term. I'm sorry to say it that strongly, but this is the great failure of evangelical Christianity. We have had Jesus without the Kingdom of God, and therefore have literally done Jesus in.[4]

That's a strong statement: If I don't know what the Kingdom of God is, I don't really know anything about Jesus.

Of course, we know something about Jesus. That's not what Fee is saying. We can know the facts about Jesus. We can know enough to be saved through Jesus. But it is correct in the sense that we fail to rightly grasp who He really is, why He came, what His ultimate plan is, and how we fit into that plan. Without knowing what the Kingdom of God is, our understanding of Jesus is incomplete and insufficient—of Him and ourselves.

Moreover, Fee's statement about the Kingdom of God is equally true for how we understand the entire Bible. Understanding the Kingdom of God is the key to understanding the law, the church, righteousness, justice, sanctification, Christian ethics, the consummation. Everything connects to it.

If we embrace the truth that Jesus taught, that starting life now in the Kingdom of God is the foundation of all living, *both now and for eternity*, then we are off to a new and life-changing start.

---

4 Gordon Fee quoted by Patrick Schreiner in *The Kingdom of God and the Glory of the Cross* (Crossway Publishers, 2018) p. 14

THE PROBLEM

Why have so many of us missed this seminal truth? I think it has, in part, to do with how we understand our salvation and the church.

It's Not the Gospel

Here's the problem: the gospel is commonly preached as an individualistic message and promise when it should be much more than that. Over forty years ago, a young woman who would eventually become my wife and who had just been converted herself, shared the gospel with me. I had never heard it explained. It was revolutionary. But there was no mention of the Kingdom of God. I put my faith in Jesus and Jesus alone as my Savior and was saved, I was His beloved child. Salvation as it was proclaimed and received was very much about me. Just me. But there was always supposed to be more.

Mistakenly, we have confused the Kingdom of God with our salvation. However, the Scriptures don't support that. Our lives should proceed from having been saved by faith in Christ into the Kingdom of God to passionately living in and as part of that Kingdom. Consider: "The time is fulfilled, and *the kingdom of God is at hand*; repent and believe in the gospel" (Mark 1:15. emphasis added).

Jesus is NOT saying that the Kingdom and the gospel are the same. He is saying that the time of the Kingdom, the reign of the king, and the people of the Kingdom are at hand. What do we need to do? Repent and believe in the saving work of Jesus, of course. But what happens then? We enter into the Kingdom.

In one sense, the gospel is the doorway into the Kingdom. Jesus said as much to Nicodemus when he asked Jesus about how to be born again. Jesus responds: "Truly, truly, I say to you, unless one is born of water and the Spirit, *he cannot enter the kingdom of God*" (John 3:5, emphasis added).

Do you see the point? He was talking about the need to be inside the Kingdom of God. When we are saved, born again, we enter the Kingdom of God. The goal was getting into the Kingdom, not being born again.

What this passage says is don't just think that you are saved from your sins. Don't just think you are justified. Don't just be amazed at saving grace. Realize that you have entered into the Kingdom of God. That's the center of gravity according to Jesus.

The Kingdom and the gospel: the two are inextricably linked. The gospel is the means of entry into the Kingdom of God. The Kingdom of God is built upon the reception of the gospel.

It's Not the Church

We might think that the Kingdom of God means the church. It doesn't.

I love the church even with all its flaws. I've held a high view of the church for decades, which the Bible calls for. The church is the bride of Christ. It is the beloved of our Savior. It is the household of God. All good and true. But the church is not the Kingdom of God.

The Kingdom of God is more than the church. As we will see in Chapter 2:

- Most importantly, it is the reign and rule of the King.
- The Kingdom of God is also more than the church; it includes angels.
- Finally, it is the Kingdom of God and its ethos, not the church, that provide the framework for knowing how to live in the Kingdom and in the world the way the King wants us to.

Moreover, we saw earlier that the Kingdom, not the church, is the great inheritance. It, not the church, is a matter of power. (I Corinthians 4:20 and Hebrews 12:28) The Kingdom is something "more" than the church.

17

Think of the church this way: We know that the church is the bride of Christ. But there is a difference between being a bride and a groom and living life as a married couple. In the case of our faith, the church, the bride of Christ, gives us some of the context for living life here on earth but it doesn't answer the question of how to live that life fully. The King and the Kingdom of God do.

CONCLUSION

Geerhadus Vos says the Kingdom of God is, "the center of gravity in his [Jesus's] preaching, that to which he attaches supreme importance… "[5]

"The center of gravity"

"Supreme importance"

It was Jesus's passion and purpose. And it should be ours.

Over many years, I have had a steady and wonderful diet of teachings pertaining to the gospel of salvation and a "cross-centered life" in which the cross of Jesus is declared to be the touchstone for how we live. It is largely rooted in personal sanctification and church life. I've met my Savior again and again through those messages. I've loved and love the doctrines of grace. The life, death, and resurrection of Jesus is a wonderful treasure. But, despite the centrality of the Kingdom in Jesus's teachings, I can count the sermons I've heard on the Kingdom of God on one hand. And that means my diet of biblical teachings has been incomplete and insufficient.

Jesus's teachings call us to live a Kingdom-centered life, not a gospel-centered life. There is a King to love and obey. There is a realm to occupy. It is far more than personal sanctification and church life, although those are very much part of the Kingdom-centered life. It

5 Geerhadus Vos, *The Teaching of Jesus Concerning the Kingdom of God and the Church*, 1903 (Reprinted 2017 by Fontes Press) p. 22

is a way to view everything, from the smallest detail of our life to the entire world around us. There is a Kingdom ethos that emerges from Jesus's teachings and it grounds our understanding of topics such as righteousness, justice, poverty, race, and how to live in this world. The outcome of the gospel as we know it (saved by faith alone, in Christ alone, through grace alone) is actually a Kingdom-centered life. One that we are to be passionate about.

If this book is successful, it will provoke a radical change in your mind and heart and in how you approach the remainder of your life here. It should change your view and affect how you live:

- It should affect how you view and treat others, especially those who are different from you.
- It should stir a passion for justice.
- It should shape your view on politics.
- It should affect how and where you spend your money.
- It should affect your understanding of marriage and children.
- It should affect how you work.
- It should affect how you preach the gospel.
- It should mediate fears and anxieties.
- It should rearrange your goals and ambitions.

So my prayer is that we all will live not just in the good of our personal salvation, not just in our comfort of being part of the church, but we all will be newly thrilled and overjoyed at realizing just how big our salvation is because we are a part what the Lord's passion is—His Kingdom.

A simple question but a profound one: *What is the Kingdom of God and why does it matter?* Now let's answer the question, embrace it, and let it change our lives.

2

A Kingdom Definition and a Kingdom Worldview

THE KINGDOM OF GOD. How hard can it be to find a common definition among theologians?

Turns out, it's quite hard. And that is a problem because if we can't define the Kingdom, how can we grasp its importance and live in it the way Jesus wants?

Commentators, theologians, and teachers have debated and disagreed on the definition of the Kingdom of God for the entirety of the church's history. The Church Fathers had multiple interpretations. The Westminster Confession of Faith calls the church the Kingdom of the Lord Jesus Christ (Chapter 25.2.ii) John Calvin, like Luther, spoke of a two-kingdom paradigm in mankind in which the "invisible kingdom" is the Kingdom of God in the believer; it is "spiritual, whereby the conscience is instructed in piety and in reverencing God" (Institutes 3:15:19). Other theologians have defined it as the sovereignty of God. For example, Martin Lloyd Jones says, "The Kingdom of God … is the rule of God; it is the reign of God."[6]

As I said, not so easy …

6 Martin Lloyd Jones, *The Kingdom of God*, (Crossway Books, 1992) p. 21

Because of the wide-ranging explanations and descriptions of the Kingdom of God in the Scriptures, particularly the New Testament, George Eldon Ladd helps us understand this panoply of definitions:

> Our problem, then, is found in this three-fold fact. (1) Some passages of scripture refer to the Kingdom of God as God's reign. (2) Some passages of refer God's Kingdom as the realm into which we may now enter to experience the blessings of His reign. (3) Still other passages refer to a future realm which will come only with the return of our Lord Jesus Christ into which we shall then enter and experience the fullness of His reign. Thus, the Kingdom of God means three different things in different verses. One has to study all the references in the light of their context and then try to fit them together in an overall interpretation. And so the diversity of definitions. When describing God's Kingdom, the Scriptures can talk about a king, a place (often seen in the Old Testament), a people, a time (already but not yet fully), and a way of life.[7]

And that doesn't begin to get into the millennial question. I leave that for others …

Following Ladd's explanation, for the purposes of this book, the scriptures speak of the Kingdom of God as having three elements:

1. The rule of the King.

2. The realm of the King, which includes subjects and place.

3. The reign of the King in the life of the subjects of the Kingdom.

Furthermore, the Scriptures also indicate that:

• *The Kingdom was foretold throughout the Old Testament.* For ex-

7 George Eldon Ladd, *The Gospel of the Kingdom*, (The Paternoster Press, 1959), p. 22

ample, the prophet Daniel speaks of the coming of the Kingdom of Heaven that will never be destroyed. "And in the days of those kings the God of heaven will set up a kingdom that shall never be destroyed, nor shall the kingdom be left to another people. It shall break in pieces all these kingdoms and bring them to an end, and it shall stand forever." (Daniel 2: 44). It won't be one of many kingdoms. A time would come in which it will stand alone. See also Psalm 45:6 and Isaiah 9:7.

- *The Kingdom began with Jesus's death, resurrection, and ascension.*
- Philippians 2: 9-11 says: "Therefore God has highly exalted him and bestowed on him the name that is above every name, so that at the name of Jesus every knee should bow, in heaven and on earth and under the earth, and every tongue confess that Jesus Christ is Lord, to the glory of God the Father." The Kingdom, while foretold in the Old Testament, was inaugurated with Jesus's life, death, resurrection, and ascension. See also Ephesians 1: 20-23.

- *The Kingdom is already operative in heaven.* Ephesians 1:20-23 says: "He [God] worked in Christ when he raised him from the dead and seated him at his right hand in the heavenly places, far above all rule and authority and power and dominion, and above every name that is named, not only in this age but also in the one to come. And he put all things under his feet and gave him as head over all things to the church, which is his body, the fullness of him who fills all in all." God the Father has given Jesus all authority and Jesus is already ruling as the head of the Kingdom now. See also Matthew 28:18, John 3:35, and Revelation 1:5.

- *The Kingdom is here on Earth already but through the internal reign of Jesus in the life of all believers.* Luke 17: 20-21 says: "Being asked by the Pharisees when the kingdom of God would come, he answered them, "The kingdom of God is not coming in ways that can be observed, nor will they say, 'Look, here it is!' or 'There!' for behold, the kingdom of God is in the midst of you." While Old Testaments Jews and Jews of Jesus's generation had been expecting a single, cataclysmic conquest by the Kingdom of God, Jesus tells us it will come a different way—internally, in the hearts of believers.

- *The time is coming when the King returns to earth and completes the establishment of His Kingdom over all creation.* Revelation 21: 1-4 says: "Then I saw a new heaven and a new earth, for the first heaven and the first earth had passed away, and the sea was no more. And I saw the holy city, new Jerusalem, coming down out of heaven from God, prepared as a bride adorned for her husband. And I heard a loud voice from the throne saying, 'Behold, the dwelling place of God is with man. He will dwell with them, and they will be his people, and God himself will be with them as their God. He will wipe away every tear from their eyes, and death shall be no more, neither shall there be mourning, nor crying, nor pain anymore, for the former things have passed away.'"

A DEFINITION

A good, concise definition comes from Patrick Schreiner: "The kingdom is the King's power over the King's people in the King's place."[8]

He credits Graeme Goldsworthy, who authored a similar albeit longer definition:

> What is the Kingdom of God? The New Testament has a great
> deal to say about "the Kingdom" but we may best understand

8 Patrick Schreiner, *Ibid*, p. 18

this concept in terms of the relationship of ruler to subjects. That is, there is a king who rules, a people who are ruled, and a sphere where this rule is recognized as taking place. Put in another way, the Kingdom of God involves:

(i)   God's people

(ii)   in God's place

(iii) under God's rule. [9]

However, as we saw in the above scriptures, the Kingdom of God is broad, rich, nuanced, and layered. For that reason, building on Schreiner and Goldsworthy, for purposes of this book, we offer this fuller definition:

> The Kingdom of God is the loving, righteous, wise, and just rule and reign of Jesus Christ, the King, over a realm that includes all believers and angels. It was foretold and foreshadowed in the Old Testament and inaugurated by Jesus's ascension to heaven after His resurrection. It is now in force fully in heaven, while here on earth it is present in and through all true believers through the agency of the Holy Spirit. It expresses the glorious qualities of the King, which is the basis for the ethos for all behavior in the Kingdom. Jesus patiently waits for the completion of the gospel to fill the final roll of citizenry of the Kingdom, at which time He shall complete his rule over all of creation by returning to earth and creating a new heaven and new earth where He will dwell with his people.

9 Graeme Goldsworthy, *The Goldsworthy Trilogy: Gospel and Kingdom, Gospel and Wisdom, The Gospel in Revelation* (Paternoster Press, 2000) pp. 53-54,

You may have read this chapter and thought, so what? Is a definition so important? Yes! In all ways!

The Basis for Our Worldview

In high school, I learned a word that has stayed with me ever since—*weltanschauung*. It is German for "worldview." It carries the idea that we understand the world and humanity a certain way. It leads to political and sociological theories, ideologies, and ways of life. It is a framework by which someone or a group of people understand and make sense of life and existence and live accordingly.

And everyone has a worldview.

A definition begins to shape (or reshape) our *weltanschauung*, our worldview. And it's important as a Christian to have a clearly defined worldview because there are so many competing and aggressive worldviews vying for our attention and our hearts: secular humanism, classical liberalism, alt right conservatism, American exceptionalism, socialism in all its flavors, modern communism, New Age religions, pluralism, post-modernism—the list goes on and on. These worldviews stand at the door of our hearts and minds and call us to follow them.

The Active Appeal of Worldviews

The book of Proverbs is helpful in understanding the active appeal of these other worldviews. In Proverbs 9: 13-18, the woman Wisdom and the woman Folly are presented calling out to the passerby.

> Wisdom has built her house; she has hewn her seven pillar. *She has sent out her young women to call from the highest places in the town*, "Whoever is simple, let him turn in here!" … The woman Folly is loud; she is seductive and knows nothing. She sits at

the door of her house; she takes a seat on the highest places of the town, *calling to those who pass by, who are going straight on their way* (emphasis added).

It is this way with worldviews. They are always calling out to us. The question becomes, what is yours?

If we coast through our life intellectually and spiritually, indifferent to the claims and appeals of opposing worldviews with no countervailing way to think biblically about all of life, those worldviews will seep into our minds and hearts, in whole or in part, and they will change us. Instead of being actively engaged in and devoted to the Kingdom of God as the great treasure and passion of our lives, we wind up with, at best, a mixture of worldviews that both compromise our life in Jesus and pull us away from Him and, at worst, lead us to oppose to the King.

The Homemade Worldview

You may say, "Well, I am not communist. Or a socialist. Or a post-modernist." And that is probably true. Most people don't assume a classic worldview. Instead, at least in the United States, we tend to absorb views and ideas from a multiplicity of worldviews. Call it "The Homemade Worldview". We toss in a bit of socialism with a bit of capitalism with a bit of humanism with a bit of post modernism, a dash of Christianity, and voila! Homemade Worldview.

Sounds funny but it is actually a dangerous homebrew to the careless Christian. If we do not tend to how we think about the world, the world will be quite happy to provide the ingredients for a contra-worldview, and that will derail how we live to the glory of God.

Here are two examples. For many Christians living in the United States, their worldview can be summarized as "Cross and Country" or "Christian Nationalism". Matthew McCullough describes Christian Nationalism as "an understanding of American identity and significance held by Christians wherein the nation is a central actor in the world-historical purposes of the Christian God."[10] It is a fusion of Christian faith and national patriotism as a single worldview. It can include the idea that the United States stands as the best example of the Kingdom of God and that we should defend the core values of the United States as much as we would defend the Kingdom itself. There are many variations of this worldview but you get the point.

A second example of a homemade worldview is the social gospel. This worldview seeks to apply Christian values to social issues such as poverty, race, and the climate. While many of its goals were praiseworthy (who doesn't want to eliminate poverty?), many adherents either reject the notion of individual salvation as critical to the gospel or elevate the transformation of the social order above individual salvation. Liberation theology can be said to come under the umbrella of the social gospel. This strain of thought spread through South America. It argued that the Bible spoke mainly through the poor and advocated a struggle by the poor against the wealthy.[11] Again, there are many variations of this worldview but you get the point.

Just in case, here is the point: Homemade worldviews that attempt to fuse the Kingdom of God with something else become a half-truth. The danger of half-truths is that they deceive people into thinking that the half-truth is true in its entirety. These attempts to "add" to a Kingdom of God worldview actually corrupts a correct

10 Matthew McCullough Cited by Thomas Kidd, "Christian Nationalism vs. Christian Patriotism", December 19, 2020 https://www.thegospelcoalition.org/article/christian-nationalism-patriotism/

11 Encyclopedia Britannica, https://www.britannica.com/topic/liberation-theology

understanding the Kingdom of God as a worldview. It is fair to say that when we conjoin the Kingdom of God with anything else (patriotism, ideology, etc.), we wrongly and dangerously and sacrilegiously reduce the Kingdom of God from what God intends it to be to us.[12]

CONCLUSION

Let's be clear—a definition is just the start. So is a worldview. And they are not enough if we are to have a compelling vision.

Take the definition of "whale" for example. The Miriam Webster definition of a whale is:

> any of various very large, aquatic, marine mammals (order Cetacea) that have a torpedo-shaped body with a thick layer of blubber, paddle-shaped forelimbs but no hind limbs, a horizontally flattened tail, and nostrils that open externally at the top of the head.[13]

That's the definition. Zzzzz, right? But if you have ever seen a whale for real in the ocean, it is a totally different experience. Seeing this immense creature gliding with ease through the water. Watching it dive and stay underwater for what seems like forever. There is a sense of awe. It is thrilling. It is a little bit scary. That's a compelling vision.

It's that way with the Kingdom of God.

Jesus wasn't passionate about a definition or even a worldview. He was passionate about something that was real and wonderful and amazing and textured and perfect. Thrilling. And a little bit scary.

---

12 This is not to say that patriotism is wrong. Or that social justice is wrong. What is wrong conjoining them to the Kingdom of God in importance as a worldview. They are, at best, secondary viewpoints.

13 Miriam Webster Dictionary, https://www.merriam-webster.com/dictionary/whale

To have some idea of what Jesus was compelled by, we have to have some idea of what the Kingdom of God is really like. We have to think about the King. The people. And we need to have an idea of what it is like to live here and now in the Kingdom.

The rest of this book tries to do that.

3

The King of the Kingdom
and the Challenge

WHILE OUR DEFINITION OF THE Kingdom of God includes the people of the Kingdom and the place of the Kingdom, it is the King who makes the Kingdom. It is the King who reigns over His territory, who decides who enters, and who determines what the Kingdom and its subjects are like. The King matters most.

That means we need to understand who Jesus the King is. And what our response to him must be.

It's not as easy as we think because our Western, twenty-first century minds face a challenge. Many of us know Jesus as Savior but we don't know Jesus as King.

THE CHALLENGE

The scriptures make clear that Jesus is King:

> Therefore God also has highly exalted Him and given Him the name which is above every name, that at the name of Jesus every knee should bow, of those in heaven, and of those on earth, and of those under the earth, and that every tongue should

confess that Jesus Christ is Lord, to the glory of God the Father. (Philippians 2: 9-11)

In heaven, this is a present reality. Saints and angels bow down and worship and obey him. But here on Earth, do we really bow before Jesus the King? Will we? Really?

In the West, particularly in the United States, we have no relatable, contemporary concept of kingship. That lack inhibits our understanding and relationship to Jesus, our King.

Three phenomena create this challenge.

Political History and Ideals

The United States, in its two hundred and forty-plus years of existence, has never had a king. Politically, we are a democratic republic. Citizens elect their leaders. Culturally, we celebrate and treasure our individual freedoms. The notion of a single supreme ruler who has absolute claim over how we live our live is, frankly, anathema to who we are as citizens of the United States.

Take for example, the debate over how to respond to the coronavirus that was raging in 2020 in the United States. A particular issue illustrates this country's aversion to being told what do to: wearing masks to moderate the spread of the virus. Millions of Americans simply refused to follow the guidance (not the orders but simple guidance) of health officials and government leaders to wear masks and did so out of the conviction that the government should not be telling them how to live their lives. In the words of one US Senator while running for office:

I'm not for the government telling us what to do … I think that we need to be wearing masks. I think that we need to be socially responsible. I think we need to understand this is a very serious situation that we're in … But I don't like the government telling us what we have to do. Surely to goodness, we can protect our own selves without the government dictating every move that we make.[14]

This is nothing new. Be it the rugged individualism as the country was settled in the 1700's and 1800's or the counter culture of the 1960's, to the rise of anti-authoritarian groups on the political left and right in the early 2000's, resistance to government authority has long been a hallmark of American culture. It's in our political DNA. It is not in our American nature to surrender our will in obedience to those in authority. As the official motto of New Hampshire says, "Live free or die."

All of this anti-authoritarianism runs counter to the Kingdom's culture that calls us to obey the King of the Kingdom of God. To willingly and totally submit to a king, in particular to a ruler who demands our complete love, loyalty, and obedience is all the more difficult for modern Americans, even American Christians. Because we are our own kings.

Twenty-First Century Pursuit of Happiness

Furthermore, at the end of the twentieth century and in the beginning of the twenty-first century, we live all the more for ourselves and our happiness.

The spirit of the Declaration of Independence and the inalienable right to the "pursuit of happiness" has never been more embraced in the United States. Be it the pursuit of sexual pleasure, the decriminalization

14 Tommy Tuberville, Interview with AL.com, July 15, 2020, https://www.al.com/news/2020/07/tommy-tuberville-maybe-to-doug-jones-debate-and-no-to-mandatory-masks.html

of marijuana, the reverent worship of sports, the craving for the latest release of the blockbuster movies, the explosion of online gaming—on and on—this is a society that has deified the pursuit of happiness.

We act as we want. We say what we want, how we want. We marry and divorce as we want. We drink and take drugs as we want. We engage in sexual relations as we want. We eat as we want. The pursuit of leisure and pleasure has fewer and fewer boundaries. We make up our own rules.

Absolute morality has given way to homemade morality, just like that homemade worldview in Chapter 2, which is more than a casual connection. Accordingly, rules and rulers have less and less sway in our minds and hearts.

Lack of a Real-Life Model of Kingship

On top of this political and cultural phenomena, our notion of kings in general is informed either by the figurehead status of kings (and queens) à la Great Britain or in the fictionalized caricatures of literature. Be it the King of England, the kings in the Lord of the Rings, or King Arthur, we have a hard time translating any notion of biblical kingship into actionable motives and behavior towards a real king.

I think many Christians are in for quite the culture shock when they arrive in heaven. Just think for a minute of a Christian who has lived fighting authority in this lifetime suddenly being confronted with the absolute King of the Kingdom of God. Do we honestly believe such a person can turn on a dime relative to absolute authority? What an abrupt and immediate change in behavior that person will experience. (Seriously, shouldn't we expect a rather long orientation class starting on the day we die?)

If heaven will present a challenge for many twenty-first century Christians, how much more does this lack of clarity about submission to a king make it hard to bow before King Jesus in our lives here on Earth? It is one thing to acknowledge that Jesus is King. It is quite another thing to live in submission to the King because it is truly true.

How Do We Overcome this Challenge?

We need a much clearer picture of our King, the Lord Jesus Christ. And we must settle in our hearts that we owe him absolute love, loyalty and obedience. All are required—love for the King, knowledge of the King, and absolute obedience to the King. And they don't come easily for the reasons outlined above, as well as our own indwelling sin.

This book cannot attempt a comprehensive survey of all the qualities and truths of Jesus the King. But the following should help us to relate more lovingly, willingly, and faithfully to our King. So let's see who this King is and what He is like.

THE KING'S LINEAGE

Lineage tells us something about someone. My wife comes from Irish stock. Her grandmother was first-generation Irish here in the United States. My wife remembers stories and also was shaped by how Irish families lived—intense family loyalty, love of music, respect for parental authority, highly religious, a bit of a rebellious streak against outside authority, valuing hard work, mothers' sacrificial love for their children. The Irish don't hold a monopoly on these traits, but my wife's lineage helps me understand her.

As for royal lineage, the line of Kings bestows authenticity. The rightful heir to a throne is established by lineage not by vote or might.

Jesus has His own lineage. And it informs us that He is the rightful king as well as the type of King He is. He comes from two lines of family:

1. He is Jesus, the Son of God—the second person of the Trinity

Jesus is the eternally begotten Son. Fully God.

You may think, "Of course He is." But that idea, that Jesus is God, is declining among evangelicals! According to one survey, thirty percent of evangelicals now agree with the statement, "Jesus was a great teacher, but he was not God."[15]

Let that sink in. Thirty percent of the people who profess to hold to the Bible as the highest authority in their life, who believe that Jesus's death on the cross is the only sacrifice that removes the guilt of their sin, do not believe that He was God.

Suddenly, the lineage of Jesus the King becomes much more important.

The Apostle John writes:

> In the beginning was the Word, and the Word was with God, and the Word was God. He was in the beginning with God. All things were made through him, and without him was not any thing made that was made … And the Word became flesh and dwelt among us, and we have seen his glory, glory as of the only Son from the Father, full of grace and truth (John 1: 1-3 and 14).

The writer of Hebrews says, "He is the radiance of the glory of God and the exact imprint of his nature" (Hebrews 1:3).

The Nicene Creed puts Jesus's divinity this way:

> We believe … in one Lord Jesus Christ, the Son of God, begotten of the Father as only begotten, that is, from the essence of

---

15) Ligonier Ministries, "2020 State of Theology Survey", September 8, 2020, https://www.ligonier.org/blog/state-theology-survey-2020-results/

the Father, God from God, Light from Light, true God from true God, begotten not created, of the same essence as the Father, through whom all things came into being, both in heaven and in earth.

This is who our King is. Fully God. He was present at the beginning of all things. He is part of the Trinity, the Godhead—Father, Son, and Holy Spirit. He is active in the sovereign control of all things. He is all-seeing, all knowing, all-powerful, all wise. He is righteous and true. He isn't just loving, He is love. He is clothed in glory and splendor. He is rightly worshipped by all creation as God.

He is not like us. He is: "The LORD, the LORD, a God merciful and gracious, slow to anger, and abounding in steadfast love and faithfulness, keeping steadfast love for thousands, forgiving iniquity and transgression and sin" (Exodus 34: 6-7).

And yet …

2. He is man—in the lineage of Abraham and King David

Matthew 1 starts with the genealogy of Jesus: "The book of the genealogy of Jesus Christ, the son of David, the son of Abraham … "

Jesus's lineage also includes His human family line. In an almost matter of fact way, the Bible introduces us to Jesus as a man, a human being with a family history.

The Nicene Creed, after affirming Jesus's complete divinity, goes on to say this about Jesus:

Who for us men and for our salvation came down and *was incorporate, becoming human.* He suffered and the third day He rose, and ascended into the heavens. And He will come to judge both he living and the dead (emphasis added).

The genealogies of Jesus in Matthew and Luke trace Jesus back to Abraham and Adam, respectively. This matters because they connect Jesus to:

- Adam, the first man, to whom the promise of restoration was promised.
- Abraham, through whom God's covenant to make a people of His own was given.
- David, the greatest of Israel's kings, whose descendant would be the Messiah.

Jesus, our King, is human. He took on human form and remains so for the rest of eternity. It didn't change His Nature as God. It didn't lessen His divinity. He added humanity to who He is. And there aren't two persons within Jesus. He doesn't have a split personality. His divinity and His humanity come together in such as a way that both are maintained and yet both combine to make a single person.

Such a great and wondrous mystery. It seems impossible to us but, then, we aren't God. Only for God is this possible.

WHY DOES HIS LINEAGE MATTER?

We can frame the answer this way: the King of the Kingdom cannot be too much or not enough. If Jesus is only God, how could we relate to Him? We can love Him, obey Him, and even trust him. But He would remain "other" to us. He would be "too much." Likewise, if Jesus was just a man, we could relate to him but He would be just another one of us. He would be "not enough". This God/Man is exactly what we need.

The God/Man Shares Our Humanity

Consider what Charles Spurgeon says, concerning Jesus the King:

To be king of men, it was necessary for him to be born. He was always the Lord of all; he did not need to be born to be a king in that sense, but to be king through the power of truth, it was essential that he should be born in our nature. Why so? I answer, first, because it seems unnatural that a ruler should be alien in nature to the people over whom he rules. An angelic king of men would be unsuitable; there could not exist the sympathy which is the cement of a spiritual empire. Jesus, that he might govern by force of love and truth alone, became of one nature with mankind; he was a man among men, a real man—but a very noble and kingly man, and so a King of men.[16]

As man, Jesus the King is one of us. He knows us. In this life, he knows our weaknesses and temptations. He knows our fears. He knows us at our worst and at our best. He is not without compassion for he is one of us. He has tasted the life of man. Hunger, sadness, oppression, discouragement, joy, death. He knows aspirations and disappointments and loss, joy and celebration, friends and foes.

And in the life to come, He will lead His redeemed people in a new way of life. He doesn't simply command us as an aloof God. He is the King who rules among His people, as one of us.

The writer of Hebrews makes this human empathy clear when describing Jesus as our great high priest:

Since then we have a great high priest who has passed through the heavens, Jesus, the Son of God, let us hold fast our con-

16) Charles Spurgeon," Jesus, the King of Truth", A Sermon Delivered On Thursday Evening, at The Metropolitan Tabernacle, Newington, December 19, 1872, https://answersingenesis.org/education/spurgeon-sermons/1086-jesus-the-king-of-truth/

fession. *For we do not have a high priest who is unable to sympathize with our weaknesses, but one who in every respect has been tempted as we are, yet without sin.* Let us then with confidence draw near to the throne of grace, that we may receive mercy and find grace to help in time of need (Hebrews 4: 14-16, emphasis added).

This is such an important point. The King of all is not far off from us. He is not unapproachable. He is never distant. He is not unaffected by our human experience. He is close to us. When He commands, he does it right next to us. What He asks of us, He does so knowing our frame, our fears, our limits.

Moreover, we read in Matthew 11:29 that Jesus is "gentle and lowly in heart." What does that mean? The King's heart is not cold and aloof. His heart is warm and humble towards us. He is accessible to us in a gentle, loving way:

Jesus walked the Earth rehumanizing the dehumanized and cleaning the unclean. Why? Because his heart refused to let him sleep in. Sadness confronted him in every town. So wherever he went, whenever he was confronted with pain and longing, he spread the good contagion of his cleansing mercy. Thomas Goodwin said, 'Christ is love covered over in flesh.' [17]

The God/Man Reveals God To Us

In addition, Jesus Incarnate helps us understand who God is. Typically, we know about God's attributes—love, wisdom, holiness, omniscience, omnipotence—and we can assent to them, even put our trust

17) Dane Ortland, *Gentle and Lowly* (Crossway Publishers, 2020) p. 32

in a God like that. But Jesus presents God in human form. We can understand God in concrete form rather than God as Spirit.

For example, when God reveals Himself to Moses, He declares Himself as: "The LORD, the LORD, a God merciful and gracious, slow to anger, and abounding in steadfast love and faithfulness" (Exodus 34:15). We read a similar pronouncement in the book of Psalms: "But you, O Lord, are a God merciful and gracious, slow to anger and abounding in steadfast love and faithfulness" (Psalm 86:15). These are glorious pronouncements about the character and person of God. They bring much comfort for sure. But with Jesus, we see these qualities in a close and personal way.

Do you want to know what graciousness is? Look to Jesus and how He was kind to sinners when they didn't deserve His kindness. Do you want to know what God's compassion looks like? See how He healed those with various diseases and afflictions. Do you want to know what steadfast love and faithfulness look like? See how He ate with prostitutes and tax collectors, the outcasts of society, the unclean ones. Jesus Incarnate presents God to us in a personal, visible form. Suddenly, the person of God is personal to each of us. This is our King.

The God/Man Is The Perfect King

Our conception of Jesus the King is likewise shaped by knowing He is the Son of God. As God, Jesus the King knows all, has perfect and complete wisdom, is perfectly righteous, is perfectly just, is love, and is good. He isn't just better than us. He is the supreme good and best of everything. He is what makes good good. He is love. This is our King.

No human king is wise enough, merciful enough, loving enough, powerful enough, holy enough. But Jesus the Son of God is. As King, He brings to bear all the attributes of God Himself. In

His proclamations, we hear God's holiness, true wisdom and perfect love. What He pronounces comes from infinite good and loving compassion. His direction and judgements are perfectly righteous and good and patient and merciful. There is true justice in what He declares and in how He governs. Mystically, wondrously, He is our King the God/Man.

WHAT WE NEED IN OUR LEADERS

I have a friend who serves as an officer in the Navy. He once explained that when a new commander takes command of a ship, there is a formal ceremony in which the previous commander relinquishes command to the new commander. At that moment, all of the sailors on that ship must obey the orders of that new commander. It goes without saying. They must obey. However, while the rank of the officer requires obedience, questions remains, "Can I trust that commander?" "What kind of person is this person?"

Above everything else, people want one thing from their leaders: trustworthiness. Can I trust the one who leads? Can I trust them to make the right decisions? Can I trust them to do what is right? Can I trust them to keep us safe? Can I trust them for justice?

We will never trust in human leaders like we can trust in Jesus the King. All human leaders have feet of clay and hearts poisoned with sin. They fail in certain ways because they are human, just like you and me. It would be a mistake to put our full trust in them.

It's not that way with Jesus. He will never fail us. He will never disappoint us. We can trust Him in every single thing and always because we know what kind of king He is. He is the all-powerful, holy, all knowing, loving, and compassionate God. We can put our trust in this King. We can give this King our complete loyalty. We can love this King with our entire being. And we can obey this King.

It is a beautiful thing to know Jesus as Savior. It is even more wonderful and soul-satisfying to know and trust Jesus as King of the Kingdom of God.

THE KING REIGNS

In addition to His lineage is the idea that Jesus the King reigns.

He pronounces authoritatively and exercises control over the Kingdom of God.

We often think of a kingdom in terms of territory: the kingdoms of France and England, the Aztec and Inca kingdoms, kingdoms and empires of India. Those kingdoms were defined as much by their territory as their sovereign.

However, the key biblical concept of the Kingdom of God is the rule and reign of our sovereign, Jesus. To be sure, there is a territory in the Kingdom of God. There are a people. But in the scriptures, the King's reign is what makes it a Kingdom:

Psalm 99:1 says: "The LORD *reigns*; let the peoples tremble! He sits enthroned upon the cherubim; let the earth quake!" (emphasis added).

Revelation 19:6 says: "Then I heard what seemed to be the voice of a great multitude, like the roar of many waters and like the sound of mighty peals of thunder, crying out, "Hallelujah! For the Lord *our God* the Almighty *reigns*" (emphasis added).

When the Jesus the King reigns, He exercises His rightful rule with power and authority. A more complete idea is that He rules with total power and authority in the execution of His perfect and good will over His realm.

Jesus's Reign and God's Sovereignty

This brings us to a question that bears consideration. Is there a difference between Jesus's reign and God's sovereignty or providence? A case can be made that there is a distinction, that a clarification is needed. God's sovereignty or providence can be defined as:

> God is continually involved in all created things in such a way that he 1) keeps them existing and maintaining the properties with which he created them; 2) cooperates with created things in every action directing their distinctive properties to cause them to act as they do; and 3) directs them to fulfill his purposes. [18]

Put succinctly, God creates, sustains, and directs everything in the universe and does so to carry out His perfect will and purposes. Not a bird falls in the forest apart from God's wise, sovereign providence. No one takes a breath, thinks a thought, rises from bed or lies down to sleep. No nation rises or falls. No president is elected. Nothing happens apart from the providence of God. Everything happens under the providential control of God.

Here's the tricky part. The scriptures make clear that God has ruled the world from the beginning. God has always been sovereign: "The LORD *reigns*; let the peoples tremble! He sits enthroned upon the cherubim; let the earth quake!" (Psalm 99:1, emphasis added). This passage comes long before Jesus is born.

In Isaiah's famous vision of the God, he sees the Lord seated on a throne in the temple. And with the Lord:

---

18) Wayne Grudem, *Systematic Theology, An Introduction to Biblical Doctrine* (Intervarsity Press, 1994) p. 315

In the year that King Uzziah died, *I saw the Lord, high and exalted, seated on a throne*; and the train of his robe filled the temple. 2 Above him were seraphim, each with six wings: With two wings they covered their faces, with two they covered their feet, and with two they were flying. 3 And they were calling to one another: "Holy, holy, holy is the LORD Almighty; the whole earth is full of his glory" (Isaiah 6: 1-3, emphasis added).

Isaiah sees the Lord on a throne, high and exalted. He sees a holy King. A king active in Isaiah's time. This is God reigning over all the world, proclaiming judgement over the nations. And it comes before the coming of the Kingdom of God and the King, Jesus.

So how is the reign of Jesus the King different from the providential reign of God from all time over all things?

- Jesus's rule over the Kingdom of God is over the citizens of the Kingdom. It does not extend to those outside the Kingdom. Jesus himself talks about those who are outside the Kingdom. For example, in John 3, Jesus tells Nicodemus that one must be born again in order to enter the Kingdom of God. In Mark 12, when one of the teachers of the law gives a correct answer about the greatest commandments, Jesus tells him, ""You are not far from the kingdom of God." Jesus's particular reign in the Kingdom of God is limited to those inside the Kingdom. On the other hand, God's providential reign extends over all.

- The consequential rule of Jesus is different from God's providential rule. For example, the Kingdom is a matter of righteousness, joy, and peace in the Holy Spirit (Romans 14:17). While God's sovereign rule extends over all of creation, the reign of Jesus results in these divine graces within the Kingdom of God. Those outside the Kingdom may experience grace in some limited manner, but only those in the Kingdom of God have the full divine experience of righteousness, joy, and peace in the Holy Spirit. In other words, what we experience in the Kingdom of God under the rule of Jesus is manifestly different than what anyone experiences in the world. Jesus's will, His plans, His decrees for you and me are completely different than they are for those outside the Kingdom. They are redemptive rather than restraining, sanctifying rather than judging, disciplinary rather than punitive. His loving and patient rule teaches and directs us how to live in the Kingdom to the glory of God. Outside the Kingdom, God's sovereign rule is to restrain evil, provide common grace, and extend the offer for salvation to those who are lost.

- Someday, Jesus's reign and God's providence will be the same. It will happen on That Day when Jesus returns to judge the living and the dead. But not yet. On that day, we will not just see the King who reigns lovingly and graciously, but also the King who brings judgment to the living and the dead, who separates the wheat from the chaff, who separates the sheep from the goats. And he will create a new heaven and earth encompassing the universe over which He will reign forever.

In this sense, Jesus's reign is a particular aspect of God's providential rule. Think of common and saving grace. Common grace is extended to mankind. Saving grace is extended to believers. In a similar way, God's sovereign providence extends over all of creation while Jesus's kingly reign extends to those in the Kingdom.

Let's look at one way the King rules.

He Reigns in Our Personal Lives

So when Jesus speaks authoritatively, He speaks with absolute authority.
Uh oh …

Here's a simple question. When was the last time you decided to do something right and thought, "I'm doing this because King Jesus says to."? More likely, we do the right thing for other reasons—sometimes from a right motive, sometimes not.

For example, we obey God because we love Him. Nothing wrong with that. But what happens in those times when we don't love Him? There are times when that happens. Or what happens when His commands don't sit well with us? Or what happens when our indwelling sin wins the moment? In other words, loving Jesus is not enough to obey Him all the time in all things.

Our total and complete obedience is predicated on who Jesus is. The King. The one who reigns in our life.

Jesus expects us to obey Him because He is the sovereign King. When He calls on us to live certain ways, it is not as our savior, or as our brother, both of which are true. But when He calls on us to live a Kingdom life in this lifetime, it is a call to obey the laws and ethics of the Kingdom. And to do so lovingly. In fact, it would be right to say that our obedience should be a loving obedience to the King of the Kingdom of God.

Let's work through one example: lust. In Matthew 5, on the Sermon on the Mount, Jesus addresses adultery and lust: "You have heard that it was said, 'You shall not commit adultery.' But I say to you that everyone who looks at a woman with lustful intent has already committed adultery with her in his heart" (Matthew 5: 27-28).

When he was running for President, Jimmy Carter was mocked and ridiculed over this passage. He admitted that he had sinned by having lustful thoughts about other women. It stunned the secular world. Lust is wrong? Everyone lusts? It's natural. What a dinosaur Carter was. He was just a religious rube from Georgia. Except he got it right.

Let this set in. The King commands us not to simply not commit adultery. In His Kingdom, no one is to lust. Many religions condemn adultery. Even atheists can agree adultery is wrong. But the King and the Kingdom of God has a higher standard than adultery. The consequential rule of a holy King means that even lust is wrong. Because within that ethical command, Jesus is bringing out other Kingdom principles that we are to 1) honor each other as created in the image of God, 2) see the blessing of sex and sexual desire inside marriage, and 3) understand that desire and union in marriage points to a higher, more precious union between the church the bride and Jesus the groom.

In these days, too many of us are not used to such a moral obligation of obedience. We see ourselves as struggling with sin and temptation. We may see ourselves as responding to a call for holiness. But who sees the pursuit of holy living as something that is normative in the Kingdom of God and in loving obedience to the King?

He is the risen King. Now. For us. Every Christian on Earth today has a King and His name is Jesus. He reigns in us which means we are called to obey Him.

When we are faced with our moral choices—marriage, sex, work, leisure, property, community, etc.—it is the King we are to obey. Right now. It also goes to our politics and national loyalty. Before we vote as Republicans or Democrats or Independents, we are loyal subjects of the King of the Kingdom. Before we declare ourselves as citizens of the United States, we are loyal subjects of the King of the Kingdom. Before we submit ourselves to the authority of this world, we are bound to obey our King.

Every heart has a throne. The question we face is who sits on that throne?

CONCLUSION

There is so much more that can be said of Jesus the King. It would make a good Bible study. There's an idea: do it. It will be some of the best time you will ever spend in this lifetime.

But let's finish with these final thoughts.

There is no king like Jesus. The one who rules the eternal Kingdom of God is unlike anyone or anything else in all creation because while He is fully human he is also above creation itself. No king could be wiser, more loving, more righteous, more compassionate, fairer, and nobler. He is altogether different in the best of ways.

No king deserves more loyalty, more devotion, more trust, more love, and more obedience.

And one last thing: a kingdom reflects the qualities of the king who reigns. Consider that. The people and place of the Kingdom of God will reflect the divine nature of Jesus the King. Because being in the Kingdom of God is not a matter of rules, of do's and don'ts, of constraints. It is a realm that is animated by the many qualities of the King. It is a Kingdom of righteousness, joy, peace, love, justice, wisdom, goodness, knowledge, and pleasure in the King, one another, and the realm we dwell in.

4

The Kingdom of God—Where Is It?

LONG AGO, BEFORE THE ADVENT of personal computers and cell phones, I was a naïve and idealistic high school senior, with an emphasis on naïve. While my friends were applying to and being accepted by colleges, I decided that I would forego college and bum around the country in a VW van for a year. These days, that would be called a gap year. For me, it was called "a stupid idea."

Consider—I didn't have a van, I didn't have the money for a van, I had no concrete plans for where I would go or where I would stay, and I had no idea how to live outside my parents' house. It was a pipe dream, really, but I was convinced I was going to do it. My poor parents.

In the summer of that foolish year, my father, an officer in the Air Force, was being transferred to Europe. He suggested that I go with him and my mother and attend the University of Maryland in— wait for it—Munich, Germany! Did I want to go? Let's see. Travel in a van I didn't have with money I didn't have or live in Europe, going to school on my father's dime no less! Oh heck yeah.

And so I did. I lived in Germany for two years, attending Maryland's college extension in Munich. I was an American in Germany. It was exhilarating and life changing. I traveled extensively and came to appreciate a different way of life in Europe: the people, the food, the history, the art, the architecture, the music, the languages, the cultures, the sports, and the politics. Life opened up for me in ways I couldn't have imagined. But at the end of those two years, I came back to the United States because I was a US citizen. It was my homeland.

The realm of the Kingdom of God is not unlike my experience living overseas. In this life, we are citizens of the Kingdom of God living in another land until that day that we go home, go to Jesus, where the Kingdom is fully present. But here, now, in this life, we carry the Kingdom of God inside us, just as I carried my citizenship in the United States in my mind and heart.

George Eldon Ladd puts it succinctly: "A reign without a realm to rule in is useless."[19] So where is the Kingdom of God? And who is in it? And what is it like? Let's look at the realm.

THE REALM OF THE KINGDOM—THE PLACE AND A MYSTERY

My wife loves mystery stories. She loves trying to guess the ending. Me? Not so much.

Turns out, God loves a good mystery too. In fact, He is the master of mysteries.

If we aren't comfortable with mystery, then we can never be comfortable with God's plans. For example, in Ephesians 3, Paul reveals the great mystery of salvation, namely that the Gentiles were to be included in the plan of salvation. The uncountable members of Abraham's family, as God pointed out the stars in His promise to Abraham, were always meant to include not just the Jews but Gentiles as well: "This mystery is that the Gentiles are fellow heirs, members of

19) George Eldon Ladd, *Ibid*, p. 22

the same body, and partakers of the promise in Christ Jesus through the gospel (Ephesians 3: 6).

The Kingdom of God is another such mystery. To start with, for ages, the Jews thought that the advent of the Kingdom of God would be a singular event that took place on Earth. Consider how life is described in the Kingdom to come. In Isaiah 9: 6-7, we read:

> For to us a child is born, to us a son is given; and the govern-ment shall be upon his shoulder, and his name shall be called Wonderful Counselor, Mighty God, Everlasting Father, Prince of Peace. Of the increase of his government and of peace there will be no end, on the throne of David and over his kingdom, to establish it and to uphold it with justice and with righteous-ness from this time forth and forevermore."

In Ezekiel 37: 21-23, we read that the Lord will gather His people from among the nation to one land and there will be one king.

In Isaiah 11: 1-9, we read that a King will arise who will judge with righteousness and with fairness to all. The wolf will lie down with the lamb. The Earth will be filled with the knowledge of the Lord.

In Isaiah 65: 17-25, Isaiah declares that there will be a new heaven and earth. The past will not be remembered. There will be joy and gladness forever. The lion will eat straw like the ox.

This was the expectation of Old Testament Jews. The king would come, defeat all his enemies on earth, and transform Israel into an eternal, blessed kingdom. There would be no more weeping. It would be a kingdom of righteousness and shalom, peaceful harmony with one another and with nature. A land of plenty. A land of righteous-ness and justice. A land where neighbors would love their neighbors. The lion would lie down with the lamb.

But it turns out that the arrival of the Kingdom of God, like salvation itself, would come quite differently from what was expected. Rather than a single event, taking place exclusively on Earth, the arrival of the Kingdom of God had an initial inauguration and awaits a final completion. Again and again, Jesus declares that the Kingdom has come:

> Mark 1: 14-15 says: "Now after John was arrested, Jesus came into Galilee, proclaiming the gospel of God, and saying, '*The time is fulfilled, and the kingdom of God is at hand*; repent and believe in the gospel" (emphasis added).
>
> Matthew 12: 25-28 says: "Knowing their thoughts, he said to them, 'Every kingdom divided against itself is laid waste, and no city or house divided against itself will stand. And if Satan casts out Satan, he is divided against himself. How then will his kingdom stand? And if I cast out demons by Beelzebub, by whom do your sons cast them out? Therefore they will be your judges. *But if it is by the Spirit of God that I cast out demons, then the kingdom of God has come upon you*" (emphasis added).
>
> Mark 9:1 says, "And he said to them, 'Truly, I say to you, there are *some standing here who will not taste death until they see the kingdom of God* after it has come with power'" (emphasis added).

This is the already and not yet mystery of the Kingdom. It is already here in the sense that it has been established and is present in some manner. But it is not fully completed here on Earth. Only with the return of the King do we see the fulfillment of all prophecy concerning the complete establishment of the Kingdom of God everywhere.

The mystery continues.

If the Kingdom of God has come, where is it? Clearly, the world does not yet reflect the prophetic fulfillment in Isaiah or Ezekiel or other biblical prophecies about the end of all things.

It's in Heaven

What the Bible teaches is that the Kingdom is fully in place in heaven. When Jesus ascended, He took His place on the throne of God. In Ephesians 1, Paul writes:

> For this reason, because I have heard of your faith in the Lord Jesus and your love toward all the saints, … that the God of our Lord Jesus Christ … *raised him from the dead and seated him at his right hand in the heavenly places, far above all rule and authority and power and dominion, and above every name that is named, not only in this age but also in the one to come.* And he put all things under his feet and gave him as head over all things to the church, which is his body, the fullness of him who fills all in all (Ephesians 1: 15-23, emphasis added).

When you die and go to heaven, you don't just go to some idyllic field with sunshine and music like we see in the movie, *Gladiator*. You go to a kingdom. A place of organized activity, of creativity, of purpose, of growth and knowledge. Talents are exercised. There is much to do and it is organized and ordered and governed. It is filled with billions of citizens.

Most importantly, there is a King ruling over this Kingdom. Jesus sits enthroned in power as King in heaven. In this age and the age to come. Angels and believers are there now. It is a place of unspeakable glory. And Jesus, the King, commands and directs. The Kingdom of God is fully established in heaven.

Here on Earth

But the Kingdom isn't just in heaven! The Kingdom of God is also here. Just not the way we would expect. There is no territory. It isn't in Israel. It isn't in the United States. You cannot measure it out like land. From Rome as the seat of Western Christianity, to the Crusades, to modern day efforts to restore Israel in the name of biblical prophecies, so much blood and effort has been spent during the Christian era futilely and foolishly trying to establish the Kingdom of God here on Earth in the form of a geopolitical entity.

Here's the mystery of the Kingdom of God. In this age, the Kingdom of God on Earth is not geographically located. It is not a political entity. It is found in the heart and life of the believer. Jesus Himself tells us so:

> In Luke 17:20-21, we read: "Being asked by the Pharisees when the kingdom of God would come, he answered them, 'The kingdom of God is not coming in ways that can be observed, nor will they say, 'Look, here it is!' or 'There!' for behold, the kingdom of God is in the midst of you'."
>
> In Luke 13: 18-21, we read: "He said therefore, 'What is the kingdom of God like? And to what shall I compare it? It is like a grain of mustard seed that a man took and sowed in his garden, and it grew and became a tree, and the birds of the air made nests in its branches.' And again he said, 'To what shall I compare the kingdom of God? It is like leaven that a woman took and hid in three measures of flour, until it was all leavened'."

The Kingdom of God—the loving, righteous, wise, and just rule and reign of Jesus Christ, the King, over all believers and angels—exists in this age of the world in the heart of each believer. The Kingdom of God here on Earth is an internal presence not an external province. It is planted in us at the moment of our salvation, uniting us with God Himself through the indwelling of the Holy Spirit, and is intended to grow and grow and grow like a mustard seed or leaven throughout our lives, becoming a towering plant that all can see and be refreshed in.

Kingdom Embassies in This World

This means that for believers on earth the Kingdom is like each of us being an embassy in a foreign country.

When I was in college, it was my dream to work in the Foreign Service of the United States' State Department. My passion was international relations and I dreamed of working overseas in a US embassy. I graduated from Georgetown University with a Bachelor of Science degree in Foreign Service. But it didn't happen. To get in, you take a written exam and then an oral exam. I missed the passing grade of the written exam by three points. We never went overseas. The Lord had a different plan for us.

Had I gone overseas in the Foreign Service, this is what I would have found at any US embassy. An embassy has a special status in the country where it is located. It is regarded as the presence of its country in the country it is located in. Even though it is on foreign soil, it is considered as belonging to the country it represents. For example, Russia cannot enter the US embassy in Moscow. An attack on a US embassy anywhere in the world is considered an attack on the United States. The US is entitled to defend it as if it were Atlanta or Los Angeles or Chicago, which is why US Marines guard them. Furthermore, the embassy represents the political and economic interests of its country in that foreign land. It advocates for the positions of the US government. It engages in cultural activities that promote US culture. It is in the other country but it is not the other country.

Sound familiar? In Philippians 3: 20-21, Paul writes: "*But our citizenship is in heaven*, and from it we await a Savior, the Lord Jesus Christ, who will transform our lowly body to be like his body, by the power that enables him even to subject all things to himself" (emphasis added).

In effect, Christians on Earth today are the embassies of the Kingdom of God: our hearts, minds, bodies. The world today is not our homeland. It's not our birthright. We are citizens of another world, a Kingdom not of this world. Just as I lived in Germany for two years but was a citizen of the United States, so we live in this world but are citizens of the Kingdom of God. We are surrounded by this world and its cultures and philosophies but we live by and represent the culture of the Kingdom and live under the ethos of the King and the Kingdom of God. We project the Kingdom of God into a fallen world. And our bodies and lives are sovereign territory of the King. We are the King's embassies.

Embassies vs. Triumphalism

One of the truths about an embassy is that while it has the ability to influence another country, it cannot transform the essential nature of that country. And that is a good reminder for us.

There is a temptation to believe that our lives here will triumph over all evil eventually. Good will win out through our intervention. As we become more rational and enlightened, as we become more moral, as we end poverty and inequality, the world will eventually be transformed into a world in which reason and good will triumphs over evil. That is a key tenant of many humanists. But many Christians also think that such a world is possible if we just pray enough, if we restore the boundaries of Israel, if we just experience revival. The good guys will win.

But the Bible doesn't paint that scenario. In fact, the last days of the world described in the Bible are days of increasing darkness. Sin will increase. Mankind will become more and more estranged from God. Paul writes of this in 2 Peter 3: 1-5:

> But understand this, that in the last days there will come times of difficulty. For people will be lovers of self, lovers of money, proud, arrogant, abusive, disobedient to their parents, ungrateful, unholy, heartless, unappeasable, slanderous, without self-control, brutal, not loving good, treacherous, reckless, swollen with conceit, lovers of pleasure rather than lovers of God, having the appearance of godliness, but denying its power.

It is a grave mistake to misunderstand our purpose in this world. We don't throw in the towel because the days are getting darker. Citizens of the Kingdom of God act as salt and light. We show the love of Christ in a world where hate and hostility are on the increase. We present a different message. We offer hope and rescue and redemption. We tend to the sick. We feed the hungry. We love those who are unlovable. We love our enemies. But we won't transform the world into a world free of war and hatred and division and injustice and crime and violence. Instead, as embassies of the Kingdom of God, our lives are meant to shine ever more brightly in an increasingly dark world until that day when the King comes back. It is the King who will transform this world.

What a mystery!

The great, eternal, powerful, righteous Kingdom is already here on Earth. Just not the way we might expect. It is in us. We don't wait for it. We have it. Already. By the presence of God in our hearts. That means we have the privilege of experiencing Kingdom life already. Righteousness. Joy. Peace. Sound good? It's yours. Already. You just have to receive Jesus as your savior by faith alone and you receive it. You don't achieve it. You don't earn it. The Kingdom of God is within you.

It also means that we have the duties and callings of being Kingdom citizens here on earth. There is a way to live. It isn't the Old Testament law. It's the law of God written on our hearts, to be cherished and obeyed. For we have a king already. When it comes to who rules our lives, Christians aren't Democrats or Republicans or communists or socialists or Americans or Chinese. We are citizens of a kingdom in which Jesus, the great King, rules. Now. Today.

5

The Kingdom of God—Who is in the Kingdom?

FIRST, THE EASY ANSWER. The Kingdom of God is filled with all believers and angels. They are all in the Kingdom of God right now. Now the layered answer.

PEOPLE FROM ALL TIME ARE THERE

The Kingdom of God is filled with people. Lots of them. From everywhere. From all times.

Believers from the Bible are There

In heaven, where Jesus reigns, every believer who has passed through the veil is alive and present in the Kingdom God. Adam is there. Eve is there. Abraham is there. Lot is there. David is there. Every Old Testament Jew with saving faith is there. Every Christian is there. Peter is there. Paul is there.

Believers Since the First Century are There

Men and women from ages past are in the Kingdom of God. Believers who lived long lives are there. Believers who died young are there.

Believers who died in their sleep are there. Believers who died long, painful deaths are there. Every martyr across the ages is there. Every believer who lived out his or her life faithfully but anonymously is there. Every rich and poor believer with saving faith in Christ is there.

Believing Family and Friends Who Went Before You are There

There are many friends who have now gone on before me. Some a long time ago. Some recently. Joe. Sandi. Stan. Jason. Kathy. At my age, the list is long and growing quickly. They are in the Kingdom of God. At their funerals or in times of mourning, I've found comfort knowing that I will see them again. In heaven, of course. But while they may have passed from my sight, they didn't pass out of the Kingdom. They are there. Right now.

Believers You Did Not Expect to See are There

More amazingly: there are people you knew or read about in this lifetime who have died that you did not expect to see in heaven. They are in the Kingdom of God. What surprises there will be when we see people we thought could never be there!

Believers Who are Estranged are There

Believers who sinned against you are in the Kingdom of God. Believers you sinned against are in the Kingdom of God. Sigh, those broken relationships. Many of us have them. Sadly, there are people who have no desire to speak to me. Some for good reason. But they are in the Kingdom too. Right now. In this lifetime.

And there are also those who you could not reconcile with in this life who have gone on to heaven. They are there in the Kingdom too. Someday, you will meet them again. And you will reconcile because the King calls you to. Kingdom life precludes offense and unforgiveness. What should have happened in this life will happen later in the Kingdom.

People From Around the World are There

More layers: believers from every nation, tribe, and tongue around the world are in the Kingdom of God. Right now. They don't have to wait until they die and go to heaven.

Believers of all colors are there. Brown, black, white, yellow. Right now.

Believers from all ethnicities are there. Right now.

Believers from nations around the world are there. Germans are there. Iranians are there. Iraqis are there. Japanese are there. Egyptians are there. South Africans are there. Kenyans are there. Nigerians are there. Mexicans. Brazilians. Indians. Chinese. Cubans.

Angels

But it's not just humans made in the image of God who are in the Kingdom of God. There are angels.

Angels … created beings who serve and worship the Lord. Oh, those mysterious beings.

Angels are in the Kingdom of God. It's funny that this is often missing in books about the Kingdom of God. And yet they are described continually in scripture as being in the Kingdom and acting as agents of grace and judgment for the King.

The scriptures speak of angels again and again. This book in no way attempts an exhaustive catalog of the many references or the many types. But consider just a few passages.

Lots of Them!

First, we read that there are many angels: "But you have come to

Mount Zion and to the city of the living God, the heavenly Jerusalem, and *to innumerable angels* in festal gathering" (Hebrews 12:22, emphasis added).

Revelation 5: 11-13 speaks of the living creatures worshipping God—not just people but all the living creatures in the Kingdom of God (emphasis added):

> Then I looked, and I heard around the throne and the living creatures and the elders the voice of many angels, *numbering myriads of myriads and thousands of thousands*, saying with a loud voice,
>
> "Worthy is the Lamb who was slain, to receive power and wealth and wisdom and might and honor and glory and blessing!" And I heard every creature in heaven and on earth and under the earth and in the sea, and all that is in them, saying,
>
> "To him who sits on the throne and to the Lamb be blessing and honor and glory and might forever and ever!"

Angels. "Myriads and thousands of thousands." The Kingdom of God is populated with angels. They will live with us. Worship with us. Talk to us. Be with us. And it is not a stretch to think we will fellowship with them and be friends with them.

Different Types of Angels

There are types of angels too. We read of the seraphim in Isaiah 61:1 (emphasis added):

> In the year that King Uzziah died I saw the Lord sitting upon a throne, high and lifted up; and the train of his robe filled the temple. Above him stood the *seraphim*. Each had six wings:

with two he covered his face, and with two he covered his feet, and with two he flew. And one called to another and said: "Holy, holy, holy is the LORD of hosts; the whole earth is full of his glory!"

In Revelation 4: 6-8, we read of four, great, living creatures. Not humans—angelic beings who are eternally worshipping the Lord around the throne (emphasis added):

And around the throne, on each side of the throne, are *four living creatures*, full of eyes in front and behind: the first living creature like a lion, the second living creature like an ox, the third living creature with the face of a man, and the fourth living creature like an eagle in flight. And the four living creatures, each of them with six wings, are full of eyes all around and within, and day and night they never cease to say, "Holy, holy, holy, is the Lord God Almighty, who was and is and is to come!"

There are archangels. Michael (Jude 1:9) and Gabriel (Luke 1:19). Angels. Beings of great power. Messengers. Given power to destroy. Power to protect. Mighty warriors. And great worshippers. They are in the Kingdom of God too. Someday, you and I will walk down a crowded street and there will be saints and angels there. With us. Among us.

What an amazing place the Kingdom of God is.

HOW DOES THIS WORK IN REAL LIFE?

The implications are staggering. It redefines everything, from how we live our daily lives to big issues like race and justice.

For example, we are often pulled into worldly camps and define our relationships in terms of who is in those camps and who isn't: Democrat. Republican. Liberal. Conservative. Black. White. Brown. Educated. Uneducated. American. Iranian. Wealthy. Poor. Middle class. But these are worldly categories, and thinking and living in these categories, defining ourselves using these categories, relating to others based on these categories, are antithetical to how we, as citizens of the Kingdom of God, live and interact with God and others.

The Kingdom is filled with this amazing, wonderful countless population of people and angels. People from everywhere. You and I are part of something far, far greater than any country or group in this world. Too often, we tend to elevate our nationality or ethnic group above others. We are too proud that we are Americans. Or French. Or Russian. Or Chinese. I say too proud because national pride contains the seeds of conceit and contempt for others. But as citizens of the Kingdom, we must guard against such contempt. The believer in India is every bit a citizen with the rights and privileges of the Kingdom as a believer in the United States. And instead of welcoming and celebrating everyone in the Kingdom, we fall into worldly contempt and self-righteousness and rivalry.

This mindset has huge rewards. For example, instead of thinking American Christianity has it all figured out, American believers benefit from and grow more from a humble attitude towards believers from other nations and cultures. Christians in Africa teach us to hope in the righteous anger of God because of the many injustices there. Evil will not go unpunished. Believers in India teach us the value of the extended family, which showcases how we are all part of the family of God. And believers in all countries remind us to stay humble because no one is completely right in how they live.

In Ephesians 2: 11-19, Paul writes about the great reconciliation between Jews and Gentiles:

Therefore remember that at one time you Gentiles in the flesh, called "the uncircumcision" by what is called the circumcision, which is made in the flesh by hands—remember that you were at that time separated from Christ, alienated from the commonwealth of Israel and strangers to the covenants of promise, having no hope and without God in the world. But now in Christ Jesus you who once were far off have been brought near by the blood of Christ. For he himself is our peace, who has made us both one and has broken down in his flesh the dividing wall of hostility by abolishing the law of commandments expressed in ordinances, that he might create in himself one new man in place of the two, so making peace, and might reconcile us both to God in one body through the cross, thereby killing the hostility … So then you are no longer strangers and aliens, but you are fellow citizens with the saints and members of the household of God …

This was a particularly dreadful hostility. Consider:

- If a Jew touched a Gentile, he or she was considered unclean. Defiled. They had to go through a cleansing regimen.
- It was unlawful for a Jew to help a Gentile woman give birth because it would bring another Gentile into the world.
- The Gentiles could not enter the temple in Jerusalem. There was a Temple Warning to all non-Jews: "No stranger within the balustrade round the temple and enclosure. Whoever is caught will be himself responsible for his ensuing death."
- If a Jew married a Gentile, his or her parents would hold a funeral because they considered that child to have died.[20]

20) John Stott, *The Message of Ephesians* (Intervarsity Press, 1979) pp. 91-92

We think of the hostility between Blacks and Whites in the United States as serious. It is. And it isn't just the United States where we see this tribal or ethnic or racial hostility: Hutu and Tutsi in Rwanda, Sunni and Shiite in the Middle East, Hindu and Muslim in India. Such hostility is part of the human condition. And these are simply cousins of the hostility between Jews and Gentiles.

But now—there is no longer Jew nor Gentile in the Kingdom of God. There is no longer Black and White. There is no longer Hutu and Tutsi. Not if they are in the Kingdom of God. Instead, Jesus created in Himself one new man in place of the two, so making peace, and reconciled them as brothers and sisters and citizens in the Kingdom. That means we don't first define our relationships with each other by political party, racial makeup, ethnic origin, sex, or nationality.

Knowing you are in the Kingdom of God, by grace alone, through faith alone, in Christ alone, necessarily demands that you change how you relate to others in the Kingdom. You are part of the citizenry of Jesus's Kingdom, equally loved by Jesus and ruled by Jesus the King. All having the same rights and privileges. That's how we must start and end in our treatment of others who are likewise in the Kingdom. We can celebrate our God-given differences, which enrich the Kingdom. We can acknowledge that our different cultures and nationalities help us expand our understanding of how to live in the Kingdom. But we cannot use these differences to divide, diminish, or disqualify others from the Kingdom.

Instead, a Kingdom mentality about others demands that our first and last thoughts about each other not be shaped by our party politics or religion or color or ethnicity or nationality. It requires you to embrace others as fellow citizens whom you are supposed to love, support, encourage, and live with peacefully, harmoniously.

Black believers with whom you disagree are in the Kingdom. White believers who you think are (and may be) racist are in the Kingdom. Hispanic believers who entered the United States illegally are there. All of these believers in the world today are fellow citizens in the Kingdom of God. It means you can disagree but love. You can think differently but you must extend charity and patience. You must honor and respect even if you find yourself in disagreement. And it means you must be willing to lay down your life for them. Serve them. Help them. Love them.

Our first and last thoughts about each other must be, "He/she is a fellow citizen of the Kingdom of God. We are united in Christ, who is not just our Savior but our King, and we must watch out for and care for and love one another for we answer to the King about each other." No political, racial, or social issue trumps being fellow citizens in God's Kingdom. Not social justice, not abortion, not climate change, not wealth inequality.

No one gets to say, "Yes, but … "and give a reason why we can't care, watch out, love, be patient with, stand with, encourage, forgive, and provide for a fellow citizen. No secondary identity—party politics, racial makeup, ethnic origin—trumps the King's demand that we love one another.

CONCLUSION—WHY DOES THIS MATTER?

For too long, too many of us have lived our lives largely oblivious to this amazing Kingdom. We've lived in this world with our minds and hearts constrained by the limits of time and space as we understand them. But the Kingdom of God calls us to open our eyes and see a Kingdom that transcends time and redefines space. The King wants us to use the promises and declarations of Scripture to picture and embrace this incredible realm populated with billions of saints and innumerable, fantastic beings. This world we occupy is really just a tiny time-worn, broken down porch outside an immense and amazing palace. We can taste and see and live in the good of the Kingdom already. This is our Kingdom.

Unfortunately, we are all too often willing to live on the worn out porch instead of in the glorious palace.

To understand this better, we have to understand that there is a Kingdom ethos that guides us now.

6

What is the Kingdom Ethos?

SO FAR, WE HAVE SEEN that the Kingdom of God is Jesus's utmost, supreme passion and the "center of gravity" in His preaching. We have a working definition. We know who is in it and where it is. Now, we can answer the second part of our original question: "Why does it matter to me?"

These next chapters lay out principles, structure, and examples that can start you on a lifetime of rethinking your thoughts, attitudes, mindset, actions, and habits. The most important element of this ethos is understanding that the Kingdom's ethos reflects the qualities and character of the king.

THE KINGDOM REFLECTS THE QUALITIES AND CHARACTER OF THE KING

When we read about past historical eras, we often come across a description of the era that is attached to the person who led that era— the Victorian Age, the Elizabethan Age, the Reign of Henry V, the reign of Louis XIV. For students of history, mention these eras and a picture comes into view. The history, the politics, the culture, the zeitgeist of the times, the morals—all are captured in the era of the monarch. We do the same to some extent with certain Presidents of the United States: the Kennedy Years, the Reagan Years, and the Obama Years. In other words, the reign of the one in charge defined the times.

Something similar but far greater, more extensive, more pervasive happens in the Kingdom of God. The key to how we should live is framed by this truth: *moral life in the Kingdom of God is suffused by, guided by, and animated by the qualities and character of the King.*

Jesus doesn't just rule over the Kingdom. The moral nature of the Kingdom and its subjects is created and saturated by who He is.

All the attributes of God—holiness, love, truth, wisdom, power, righteousness, justice, unchangeableness, timelessness, omnipresence, merciful, peace, patience, beauty, and goodness—all of these and more animate the Kingdom. They are the moral ecology of the Kingdom, like the air we breathe, the water we drink, the food we eat. They determine what kind of Kingdom citizens we are and how we live in the Kingdom of God.

When it comes to the cultural and moral atmosphere of the Kingdom, we don't add anything when we become citizens. There are no missing elements to the Kingdom's moral culture—no missing wisdom, intellect, goodness, love, friendship, justice, or righteousness. The King and only the King creates that moral atmosphere.

When we enter the Kingdom, it is as perfect as it ever will be because the King is perfect. All of His decrees, teachings, choices, decisions, proclamations, and fellowship are perfect. We simply have the privilege to live in it with the King who makes it so. And not just in heaven but here. Now. For the citizens of the Kingdom here on Earth.

THE ETHOS OF THE KINGDOM

Ethos is defined in the Oxford Dictionary as "the set of moral beliefs, attitudes, habits, etc., that are characteristic of a person or group." It is the atmosphere in our hearts that animate how we choose to live morally and ethically.

For example, individual freedom is part of the ethos of the United States. "Life, liberty, and the pursuit of happiness" is part of our ethos. It's sometimes hard for Americans to see that ethos, but when people from another country come and spend any amount of time in the United States, they are quick to point out various elements of the American ethos. Freedom of speech. The opportunity to make your own life based on your own effort. Freedom of religion. On and on.

The Kingdom of God has its own ethos and that ethos reflects the King, which means how we live, the choices we make, the morals and impulses and decisions, and actions and habits are all animated by the nature of the King. I call this way of life in the Kingdom, permeated by the nature of the King, the ethos of the Kingdom.

For example, Paul makes an important statement about what the ethos of the Kingdom of God is like: "The Kingdom of God is not a matter of eating and drinking but of *righteousness, joy and peace in the Holy Spirit*" (Romans 14:17. emphasis added).

Of course, anyone anywhere can experience these things. Righteousness, the doing of what is right. Joy, the deep-seated, settled delight. Peace, the absence of conflict and the presence of harmony. Anyone can. But for the citizen of the Kingdom of God, the end of that passage is the key. For the citizen of the Kingdom, righteousness, joy and peace are found in and through the Holy Spirit. It is this God-initiated, God-sustained element of righteousness, joy, and peace that sets the ethos of the Kingdom apart from that of the world.

And the Kingdom of God is far more than righteousness, joy, and peace. Consider this list of the fruit of the Spirit, which is not meant to be exhaustive: "But the fruit of the Spirit is love, joy, peace, patience, kindness, goodness, faithfulness, gentleness, self-control; against such things there is no law" (Galatians 5: 22-23).

Each of these fruits of the Spirit has its own individual quality. But when taken together, a way of life emerges, a way of living morally, a life of particular habits, and ways of thinking. The fruit of the Spirit is part of the ethos of the Kingdom of God.

But let's be clear. The ethos of the Kingdom of God is more than the fruit of the Spirit. It means attitudes towards the King, towards others, and internal ways of thinking and feeling and acting, and attitudes and behaviors inspired and guided by the Holy Spirit and the King.

This is what life in the Kingdom of God is like. And it is something we should want and live for. Be passionate about. Commit to earnestly.

THE ESSENCE OF THE KINGDOM ETHOS

We find the foundation for a Kingdom Ethos in this simple statement by the King:

> But when the Pharisees heard that he had silenced the Sadducees, they gathered together. And one of them, a lawyer, asked him a question to test him. "Teacher, which is the great commandment in the Law?" And he said to him, "You shall love the Lord your God with all your heart and with all your soul and with all your mind. This is the great and first commandment. And a second is like it: You shall love your neighbor as yourself. On these two commandments depend all the Law and the Prophets" (Matthew 22: 34-40).

Jesus makes an extraordinary claim. All of what we know about the Old Testament depends on these two commands. Literally, they "hang on" these two fundamental moral principles:

1. Love the Lord God with all your heart and with all your soul and with all your mind.

2. Love your neighbor as yourself.

Without these two simple yet great commands, everything else in the scriptures is robbed of its heart. Paul says as much in Romans:

> Owe no one anything, except to love each other, for the one who loves another has fulfilled the law. For the commandments, "You shall not commit adultery, You shall not murder, You shall not steal, You shall not covet," and any other commandment, are summed up in this word: "You shall love your neighbor as yourself." *Love does no wrong to a neighbor; therefore love is the fulfilling of the law* (Romans 13: 8-10, emphasis added).

Here then is the essence of how Kingdom citizens are to live. All their thoughts, all their words, all their actions, all their habits must proceed from these two simple yet profound motives. Love God and love your neighbor.

THE INCREDIBLE, IMPOSSIBLE ETHOS

While it is tempting to think of the Kingdom ethos as just another moral framework, a closer examination reveals that it is unlike any other moral framework because it is rooted in and reflective of the King who is the Man/God. It is qualitatively and quantitatively above all other moral codes. In a sense, all other moral codes are pale imitations of the Kingdom ethos. And apart from Jesus's atoning work and the Holy Spirit's active involvement, we quickly see that it is an incredible, impossible ethos. Consider the Sermon on the Mount.

The Sermon on the Mount (Matthew 5-7) is one of the best known passages in the Bible. But while Jesus spoke to a large, mostly unbelieving crowd curious about this suddenly famous preacher, the sermon was and is intended for the citizens of the Kingdom of God. How do we know? Because what Jesus teaches is the incredible, impossible ethos of the Kingdom of God.

For example, Matthew 5: 21-48 speaks of anger, lust, divorce, oaths, and love for our enemies. Jesus introduces them by connecting them to the Old Testament law. Matthew 5: 20 says, "For I tell you, unless your righteousness exceeds that of the scribes and Pharisees, you will never enter the kingdom of heaven." See it? He connects what he is about to teach on with the ethos of the Kingdom of God. He says that the righteous life of the citizens of God must exceed the scribes and Pharisees of that time, who were scrupulous in keeping the laws of the Old Testament and were revered for their righteousness. But even in their case, Jesus says, "Not good enough."

Jesus proceeds to illustrate the Kingdom ethos that, upon reflection, seems impossible:

- Anger is equivalent to murder in its moral seriousness. You must not be angry (Matthew 5: 21-22).
- Lust is just as bad morally as adultery. You must not lust in your heart (Matthew 5: 27-28).
- Divorce is far more serious than the Jews thought. It must only be granted in the most extreme of instances (Matthew 5: 31-32).
- Oaths are of no value, only truth telling is. Either you lie or you tell the truth (Matthew 5: 33-37).
- Don't just love your friends, love your enemies (Matthew 5: 43-48).

Stop and think about these moral habits and actions. If you asked someone who is not a Christian, "Is this realistic? Is it possible to not lust? Is anger as bad as murder? Is divorce so bad? Can an oath make the truth more truthful? Should you love your enemy?" What would they say to you? They would look at you as if you are crazy. No one can live like that. Anger isn't as bad as murder. Lust and adultery aren't the same thing. This Kingdom ethos is impossible. Sadly, many Christians would agree. It's impossible. And they ignore it to their own peril.

But this is what moral life in the Kingdom of God is meant to be like. A moral and ethical climate like no other. Why? Because the Kingdom of God reflects the King, not us. How we live, the choices we make, the morals and impulses and decisions, and our actions and habits are all animated by the nature of the King. Life in the Kingdom of God is suffused with, guided by, and animated by the perfect qualities and character of the King.

How could our righteousness be so impossibly perfect? Because what is impossible for us is possible for the Savior/King of the Kingdom. He is the God who chose you before the beginning of time, who caused you to be born again of the Spirit, and who gave you the gift of repentance and faith. In doing so, the King took your guilt and punishment on the cross and gave you His righteousness forever so that when God looks on you, He sees the Son's righteousness. Each and every moment. Forever. This perfect righteousness is never grounded in what you do. It is founded and grounded in Jesus, the perfect Son of God. On your best day. On your worst day.

This imputed righteousness from Jesus allows us to enter the Kingdom and live out the Kingdom ethos in this life. Justified by grace alone, we live Kingdom life by grace alone, empowered by the Spirit of God. We have been rescued from the hopeless bondage of sin in the kingdom of darkness to the glorious Spirit-empowered life in the Kingdom of God. It is the Spirit who gives you grace to live the impossible ethos of the Kingdom. And it Jesus's blood that covers your sins when you don't.

Let's tease this out with some examples. When you are on social media, arguing with someone about something, this ethos should come to mind when you are tempted to take the low road. Something inside you should happen. When tempted to insult someone, call someone a fool, speak insultingly, or mock someone, an alarm should go off, "Danger Will Robinson, not Kingdom speech." Run away. More than that, read how Kingdom citizens are to treat their enemies:

> You have heard that it was said, 'You shall love your neighbor and hate your enemy.' But I say to you, Love your enemies and pray for those who persecute you, so that you may be sons of your Father who is in heaven. For he makes his sun rise on the evil and on the good, and sends rain on the just and on the unjust. For if you love those who love you, what reward do you have? Do not even the tax collectors do the same? And if you greet only your brothers, what more are you doing than others? Do not even the Gentiles do the same? You therefore must be perfect, as your heavenly Father is perfect (Matthew 5: 43-48).

How is this lived out in real life? During the increasing racial and social tensions in the United States in 2020, the country has seen right wing white supremacy groups, left wing violent radicals, and other hate groups come out into the light. We've seen the angry polarization of political parties and factions. Anger and hatred seem to be growing like few times in its history. But this anger towards political and cultural "enemies" isn't restricted to the extremes of society. Christian attorney, writer, and columnist David French notes:

We increasingly loathe our political opponents. The United States is in the grasp of a phenomenon called "negative polarization". In plain English this means that a person belongs to their political party not so much because they like their own party but because they hate and fear the other. Republicans don't embrace Republican policies so much as they despise Democratic policies. Democrats don't embrace Democratic policies as much as they vote to defend themselves from Republicans. At this point, huge majorities actively dislike their political opponents and significant minorities see them as possessing subhuman characteristics.[21]

More and more Americans feel like they are in opposing groups who are facing their enemies. Hatred for the enemy is growing and Christians aren't immune to these deadly attitudes. Christians are falling into this morass of hate and division. Doing so isn't a sociological problem for them; it is a spiritual problem. It indicates a sinful sickness within the Kingdom that must be rooted out because it violates the King's ethos. Hating your opponent, despising your opponent, seeing oneself as morally superior is an utter failure to live out the command to live as believers in the Kingdom. When Christians should be at the forefront of loving their neighbor and showing a different way to live in the United States, too many are part of the problem, not the solution. The Kingdom ethos points the believer in another direction. Love God and love your neighbor like yourself.

PACIFISM VS. THE USE OF FORCE

A brief note is required here. There has been a long historical debate over this command to love your enemies in terms of pacifism versus

---

21) David French, *Divided We Fall* (St Martins Press. 2020) p. 20

the use of force, particularly war. Put simply, does the call to love our enemy preclude the use of force?

The issue seems to be a matter of conscience. Some, like the Quakers, have foresworn the use of force in all instances. However, there is a long and rich defense of just wars going back to the church fathers.

Let it be noted that Jesus himself did not oppose the military. In Luke 3:13, when some soldiers ask him what to do, he does not say stop being soldiers. That was the moment he could have spoken out against the use of military force. Instead, he tells them to act honestly and not extort money by threats or false accusations. In other words, there is an ethical code for behavior by the military that is grounded in the Kingdom ethos. Furthermore, we read in Luke 22: 38 that the disciples themselves were armed with two swords, arguing that there is a place for self-defense against criminals. And the scriptures make clear that we inhabit a world filled with evil. By inference, one can make the case for the need for self-protection, as well as for police to serve and protect and use force when necessary. However, all behavior involving force is still guided by the commands to love God, love your neighbor, and to love your enemy. For example, stopping violent aggression with force can be rooted in love for our family and neighbors. The Kingdom ethos always guides all moral behavior.

At best, then, it seems that conscience, guided by scripture, dictates in this issue.

Let's continue to look at the framework for the Kingdom's ethos.

7

The Ethos of the Kingdom —Relating to the King

THE KINGDOM ETHOS INCLUDES A vertical aspect in how we relate to the King, a horizontal aspect in how we relate to others, and an internal aspect of how we live inside ourselves—call it our attitude about life.

In this chapter, we start with the King because our relationship with others and our own internal attitude originate from Him. The more we are rightly related to the King, the more we rightly relate to others. And the more we are rightly related to the King, the more our own internal bearings are aligned with how the King wants us to be.

HOW WE RELATE TO THE KING

What do you think the primary purpose of life is? To be happy? To live a good life? My father's stated goal was to leave things better than he found them. None of these are bad purposes. But for the Christian, the primary purpose in this life is to live to the glory of God, period: "So, whether you eat or drink, or *whatever you do, do all to the glory of God*" (1 Corinthians 10:31, emphasis added).

This is a bit tricky because as we parse this out, we see that there are different ways in which we live for His glory. For example, we know that God is our Father and we are His children. This is a wonderful way to live to the glory of God. We also know Jesus is our Savior and we are to relate to Him as Savior, another wonderful way to live to God's glory. But Jesus is also King. King of the eternal, glorious Kingdom of God. And so we look to this Kingdom ethos to relate to Jesus as King. To the glory of God.

A Kingdom ethos means that our actions, words, attitudes, and habits toward Jesus the King look a certain way. Here are four examples of a moral and ethical disposition towards Jesus the King.

1. Loving Obedience to the King.

As we've already said, one of the principle ways we relate to Jesus the King is through loving obedience to all He commands. 1 John 5:3 says: "For this is the love of God, that we keep his commandments. And his commandments are not burdensome."

In the Kingdom, our hearts have been changed so that obedience is now normative. A Kingdom ethos that is intent on glorifying the King means that we don't quarrel with Him. We don't ignore Him. We don't cherry-pick what seems good to us. We don't vote on it. There are no focus groups. We don't conduct a poll to see if the majority agrees. We hear and we obey the King. Obedience means we obey the King commands and we do what He tells us to do.

Furthermore, the King not only expects obedience but loving obedience. Born out of a love for God in our glorious salvation and adoption as His children, we obey the King's commands.

A friend once made a good observation. Children often obey their parents not because they love their parents but because they seek approval or reward or to avoid punishment or because, well, we are parents, authority figures. Do they obey because they love their parents? Not as often as we might wish.

In the case of the King, there is a new and different Kingdom dynamic by which we obey. We don't obey out of fear of God or a desire for reward or acceptance. We obey because of the great love of God has for us that causes us to love Him back in obedience. His love for us, in a sense, compels us to obey out of a loving response to Him. And we obey because we recognize that Jesus is the King. The one who is owed obedience for who He is. Hence, loving obedience.

Where do we find the King's will for us? The scriptures, with the illumination provided by the Holy Spirit, provides a lifetime of teaching on how to lovingly obey. Jesus, Himself, taught on the Kingdom, so we have His very words. We have seen how the apostles proclaimed the Kingdom of God as part of the gospel message, which means that the epistles are part of the declaration from the King about how we are to live. We know that the Old Testament likewise provides additional guidance on the King's direction. This means we need to be steeped in the scriptures if we are to know the King's heart and commands. Lack of knowledge of the scriptures is a prescription for defaulting to other worldviews and ethical norms, and with it, the failure to lovingly obey. Likewise, we need to be a people who know how to listen to the Spirit. For it is the Spirit who makes the King's commands clear.

The trouble is that while we assent to this as Christians, when it comes to actually obedience in the specifics, we pause or we completely disobey. Take divorce. Jesus the King says this: "It was also said, 'Whoever divorces his wife, let him give her a certificate of divorce.' But I say to you that everyone who divorces his wife, except on the ground of sexual immorality, makes her commit adultery, and whoever marries a divorced woman commits adultery" (Matthew 5:

31-32).[22] In spite of this command, divorce among Christians is far too common. New excuses are added without warrant—incompatibility, finding the "right" soulmate, growing apart, etc.[23] Something is wrong with that picture.

Here's an "easier" one (sic): "So whatever you wish that others would do to you, do also to them, for this is the Law and the Prophets" (Matthew 7: 12). The Golden Rule commands us to treat others the way we want to be treated. Who doesn't want to be treated with respect, courtesy, kindness, forgiveness, grace? At all times. So we should treat others. While driving. While on social media. When you are in line at the store. At work.

Loving obedience is easy until it isn't. But it's what life in the Kingdom is.

Is it hard? Sometimes. Do we get it right every time, all the time? No. But in the Kingdom's ethos, our heart's inclination is to lovingly obey. Because He is the King. And when we fail, we admit it, seek forgiveness, get back up, and try again with the grace God gives us through the Holy Spirit. That's the Kingdom ethos of loving obedience. To the glory of God.

2. Servanthood vs Being Served/Personal Independence.

While we have a fundamental identify in Christ, redeemed and adopted as children of God, the Kingdom ethos calls us to a particular

22) Paul, inspired by the Holy Spirit, adds a second reason for divorce in 1 Corinthians 7:10-13. If an unbelieving spouse will not remain with a believing spouse, he or she is free to divorce. However, even here, the goal is to avoid divorce where possible.

23) There are other situations, such as spousal abuse, that require great wisdom, and arguably permit separation. Those situations often should include church discipline as appropriate because there are sin issues that have nothing do to with marriage. Such situations can include legal authorities being involved. Those situations go beyond the point in this book, which is arguing that the reasons for divorce are extremely limited and narrow.

role: servant. And Jesus calls us to imitate Him in this way:

> But Jesus called them to him and said, "You know that the
> rulers of the Gentiles lord it over them, and their great ones
> exercise authority over them. It shall not be so among you. But
> whoever would be great among you must be your servant, and
> whoever would be first among you must be your slave, even as
> the Son of Man came not to be served but to serve, and to give
> his life as a ransom for many (Matthew 20: 25-28).

I can think of no more countercultural attitude than embracing
and living the Kingdom ethos of being a servant. It is my observation that in the United States, more and more, we act as an entitled
culture. We feel entitled to food, free education, the jobs we want, to
entertainment, the homes we want. We expect to be served, not to
serve. In our affluence, the highest goal is to be one who is served at
every turn. And those who serve? We thank God that we are not like
those who serve.

In the Kingdom of God, the highest goal is to be a servant of the
King. To live and do His will. To rightly understand that we live to
serve Him and not vice versa.

Understand that we often mistake acts of service as servanthood.
The King calls us to be servants. That means we don't put on our servant's
hat, do something for Him, then take that hat off and return to our
personal independence or our pleasures. We are servants, those who do
what our King asks of us. Jesus describes the servant's attitude this way:

> Will any one of you who has a servant plowing or keeping
> sheep say to him when he has come in from the field, 'Come
> at once and recline at table'? Will he not rather say to him,

'Prepare supper for me, and dress properly, and serve me while I eat and drink, and afterward you will eat and drink'? Does he thank the servant because he did what was commanded? So you also, when you have done all that you were commanded, say, 'We are unworthy servants; we have only done what was our duty' (Luke 17: 7-19).

"Unworthy servants." "We have only done our duty." When was the last time we said that to the Lord? It's a long way from the American sense of entitlement and self-love.

3. Dependence on the King vs Self-Independence.

One of the sociological and psychological hallmarks of Western culture, is self-sufficiency, the idea that we can control our lives and we as individuals can do it on our own.

For much of the history of the United States, this self-independence and self-reliance largely was externally focused. Be it Horatio Alger stories, John Wayne, the Marlboro Man, or Marvel Comic's Iron Man, the notion of the strong, independent man has been a core value of the American ethos. In the movie, *Armageddon*, Bruce Willis is that type of solitary hero. Given the challenge of destroying a world-killer asteroid, he lands on it with his oil drilling crew, who must drill a deep hole, place a nuclear bomb at the bottom, and then blow up the asteroid before it hits Earth. He stoically faces challenge after challenge on his own. Only at the very end, when it seems that all is lost, does he call out to God and asks, sardonically, for "a little help." This is the great American hero. We face the world on our own and strive to conquer it on our own.

In the late 1900s and early 2000s, in addition to the self-dependency of the past, a psychological and emotional self-reliance has taken its place in the American ethos. In Simon and Garfunkel's iconic song "I am a Rock," we hear these lyrics:

> I've built walls
> A fortress deep and mighty
> that none may penetrate
> I have no need of friendship, friendship causes pain
> its laughter and it's loving I disdain
> I am a rock
> I am an island[24]

This is the anthem of our times. As the extended family becomes rarer, especially in White families, as families fracture, as people become less and less rooted, as local communities become less community and more a collection of personal castles, as the idea of mutual dependence declines, the American ethos is a lonely one. Even among those who long for community, loneliness pervades the culture. And it shuns the idea that we should depend on the King of the Kingdom.

The Bible declares a very different way of life. In the Kingdom of God, its citizens depend on the King for everything. We know that in Him, we live and move and have our being (Acts 17:8). Job 10:12 says, "In his hand is the life of every living thing. He gives to all life and breath and everything (Act17:25). We are called to lean on God in all things in all ways at all times (Proverbs 3:5). We are told to pray without ceasing (1 Thessalonians 5:17). We derive our wisdom from God (James 3: 13-18). We know that the King is at work in all things and controls all things. And so we relate to the King in humble dependence.

24) I Am a Rock lyrics ©1966 Paul Simon Music, Lorna Music Co Ltd,

4. Gratitude/Thanksgiving towards the King vs Self-Pity.

In the Kingdom, citizens express gratitude in all things towards the King. A grateful heart is the foundation of how we relate to the King. As Paul writes: "Rejoice always, pray without ceasing, *give thanks in all circumstances*; for this is the will of God in Christ Jesus for you" (1 Thessalonians 5: 16-18, emphasis added).

Thankfulness and gratitude … it should be a constant in our lives.

- As we are increasingly aware of who the King is.
- As we are increasingly aware of all He has done, is doing, and will do for us.
- As we see the King ordering the sun to rise in the morning and set at night.
- As we understand that every single breath we take is by the loving order of the King.
- As we see the King behind our prosperity.
- As we are aware of the intimate love of the King in our heart.
- As we feel the presence of the King in the midst of our great trials and tragedies and sufferings.
- As we come to treasure our great salvation and understand in greater measure how it is by grace alone, through faith alone, in Christ alone.

The opposite of thanksgiving? Ingratitude. Complaining. Grumbling. It is so natural in this world to grumble and complain about things big and small in life. We can grumble about the traffic. We can complain about the weather. The list is as long as everything in our lives. We can be ungrateful for what we don't have. But if, in fact, it is the King rules who over your life, who provides for your very life and breath, then any grumbling or complaining is ultimately towards the King Himself. We may not name the King by name, but we are expressing our displeasure towards Him for the King-allowed condition we find ourselves in.

There is only one response to life under the King—thanksgiving poured out from our hearts and lips to Him. In a life filled with moment-by-moment gratitude, there is no room for ingratitude, self-pity, or discontent. Only thanksgiving and gratitude. Even in moments of great suffering, the citizen of the Kingdom doesn't forget to offer his or thanks to the sovereign King who is leading them through that suffering. One can never be thankful or grateful enough towards the King.

How will you respond when your days are filled with riches and success? It seems easy to be thankful for our prosperity but that is often not the case. We take our prosperity for granted and fail to thank the King for what He gives us. Others fall into the temptation of being grateful for the gifts but not the giver of the gift.

How will you respond when the days turn dark? When you become sick? When your loved ones become sick? How will you respond when others around you are angry because their candidate wasn't elected? It's easy to be thankful when things are going well. How will you respond when you don't get that job or promotion that you think you deserved? It is a test of your thankfulness when they don't go well.

Remember Paul's words: "Be thankful in all things." Do you hear the King's voice behind that? In the Kingdom's ethos, thanksgiving and gratitude are axiomatic.

These are just four illustrations of a Kingdom ethos and how we are to relate to the King. There are so many other ways. For example:

Worship of the King vs. Self-Exaltation

We are called to celebrate and adore the King (Psalm 29:2, 95:6, 99:5, etc). The scriptures are filled with calls to praise the Lord, the King. Every day. And true worship is both a matter of the heart and the life lived. Our lives here on Earth should reflect a state of worship towards the King of the Kingdom, day in and day out. This is in contrast to the idea of celebrating ourselves, ignoring the King or relegating Him to an hour a week in church with just a few songs. This notion of self-exaltation, which is rampant in Western culture is the very antithesis of how we should live in the Kingdom.

Friendship with the King

Unlike the royalty we read of and see in the media who remain aloof and distant from commoners, Jesus is both King and friend. He is the friend of "tax collectors and sinners" (Matthew 11:29). Dane Ortland writes, "Here is the promise of the gospel and the message of the whole Bible: In Jesus Christ, we are given a friend who will always enjoy rather than refuse our presence."[25] From the beginning in the Garden of Eden, the sovereign God who created everything and everyone meant to walk in the cool of the garden with each of us as the best of friends. We were made to know Him and be known by Him, to enjoy one another, to trust and respect each other, and carry a deep affection for each other. The Kingdom ethos calls us to spend intimate time with this king. As friends.

Trusting the King vs Worry

The King expects us to trust in Him with our whole heart and not lean on our own understanding (Proverbs 3: 5-6). He expects us to believe and rely upon His sovereign rule in our life and in the world. Rather than worry over what may come, we rest in the powerful, loving, knowing power of the King. When we truly embrace the complete rule of the King, knowing Him to be loving, all wise, just, and holy, we begin to free ourselves from worry and anxiety.

25) Dane Ortland, *Ibid*, p. 115

Loving the King vs Loving Ourselves

There are many reasons to love God. One of them is because of the kind of King that He is. As we've seen, He is not far off; rather, he is close to us. He is not indifferent to us in our weakness. Rather, He has lived a human life and knows our hearts. He is just and wise. We know He will make all things right in His time. But the greatest reason to love the King is because the King loves each of us (1 John 4: 19). Dearly. Truly. With a love that is greater than any love here on Earth. The King's love transcends a father's or mother's love for their children, a husband's or wife's love for his or her spouse, a friend's love for a friend. When we stop for a minute and consider how great the King's love for us is, how can we not love Him back? Why wouldn't we love the King? How small and insignificant and embarrassingly petty self-love appears next to the King's love for us.

Self-Sacrifice for the King vs Selfishness

If we live for the King, we will live lives of sacrifice (Galatians 2:20). Loving obedience to the King means that we surrender our preferences and choices. We no longer live for ourselves and our rampant, unquenchable desires. It can be as simple as getting up in the morning to go to work or raise your children or go to church on Sundays. It can be serving your neighbor rather than watching the sports game or movie that you wanted to watch. It may mean a lesser lifestyle because you give your tithes and offerings to your church, or donate to just causes. It can be living somewhere that the King calls you to rather than living in the area of your choosing. The King, who sacrificed His life for you, calls you to live sacrificially for Him.

Humility towards the King vs. pride in ourselves—The love the King extends to us is a matter of grace. As Paul writes in 1 Corinthians 4:7, "What do you have that you did not receive? If then you received it, why do you boast as if you did not receive it?" Entering the Kingdom is a matter of grace. Living in the Kingdom is a matter of grace. Every breath we take is a matter of grace. All of the talents and abilities we have are simply due to the empowering grace of the King. There is no room for pride in the Kingdom of heaven, merely humble gratitude lived out towards the King.

CONCLUSION

There is a body of work by pastors, teachers, and theologians in the last century that brilliantly lays out the case for living our lives in light of the cross, that is, living with a daily apprehension of the saving work of Jesus. Let me append that. To be sure, it is vital to retain a love for the work of Jesus as our Savior. Living our lives here requires us to stay freshly aware of the work of Jesus in savings us. But as citizens of the Kingdom, it is equally if not more important that we face towards and live close to the throne. So in terms of living this life, it is not the cross or the throne. It's both. And we should be growing in our reverence for and awe at Jesus the King while also worshipping Jesus the Savior. Only then will we truly begin to apprehend the glory and wonder of who Jesus is.

How we relate to Jesus as King determines everything else. This worldly culture makes it extremely difficult to live out this part of the Kingdom ethos. Loving obedience, servanthood, dependence, and thankfulness towards the King are like swimming upstream against the temptations and cultural norms of self-exaltation, self-satisfaction, and self-determination.

But we have the Holy Spirit at work in us, directing us, empowering us to live the way the King has always wanted us to live. We have the cross behind us and the throne in front of us. We have a Shepherd King who cares for us moment by moment. Of course we can do it.

The Kingdom of God changes everything.

8

The Ethos of the Kingdom—
Relating to Others

THE KINGDOM ETHOS ALSO HAS a horizontal aspect, which is how we relate to others. It is the working out of the second great command, love your neighbor as yourself.

WHO IS OUR NEIGHBOR?

To live out the Kingdom ethos, we must remember Jesus's answer to the question, "Who is my neighbor?" Too often, we forget that answer and, in doing so, fail at the command to love our neighbor.

When asked that question, Jesus told the parable of the Good Samaritan. A Jewish man goes out on a road from Jerusalem to Jericho. The listener at that time would have known that road. It wasn't safe. Sure enough, the man is robbed and beaten and stripped and left for dead on the side of the road. So there he was—helpless, naked, and dying. By the side of an unsafe road. Alone. After some period of time, a Jewish priest walks by. He doesn't stop. He passes by, very likely because the man had been so badly beaten that he was bleeding and the priest would have become ceremonially unclean by coming in contact with the man's blood. Next, a Jewish Levite, a member of the priestly class, walks by. He doesn't stop either, also because of becoming unclean. Two men of his own people, ostensibly the most righteous people among the Jews, temple-going people, don't stop to help. They were observing the Mosaic law of cleanliness but ignoring the greater command to love their neighbor.

Later, another man comes along. A Samaritan …

Before proceeding, we need to understand what Jesus introduces with a Samaritan. Samaritans were a mixed population of Jews and Gentiles. They shared a common ancestry but worshipped in different places and with different views of God. Jews and Samaritans were antagonistic towards each other and often engaged in violence. Jews considered that any contact with Samaritans, even drinking from the same water well, made them unclean and, therefore, had to ceremonially cleanse themselves when they came in contact with each other.

So a Samaritan in the parable would have immediately captured Jesus's Jewish listeners' attention. When the Samaritan sees the man, a Jew, he stops. He tends to the man. He dresses his wounds. And not only that, he puts the Jew on his own donkey and takes him to an inn where he pays to have the man cared for. The Samaritan gives the innkeeper two denarii, the equivalent of a day's wage.

Who loved his neighbor? Not the priest. Not the Levite. Not the devout, church going fellow members of his race. It was the Samaritan.

Jesus, in a simple parable, redefines for all of us who our neighbor is. It's not just those who live next door. It's not just other Christians. It's not just those who are the same race or citizens or tribe or political party. Your neighbor is your fellow man or woman. And the King commands us to love our neighbor. Not just wish them well. Not just to sympathize. Love them. Like you love yourself. In fact, Jesus is not just identifying who our neighbor is but what it looks like to love your neighbor. Love them as you love yourself. Can you hear that? Loving your neighbor is costly. In time. In money. In comfort and ease. The King says this is your ethos now.

Suddenly, the command to love your neighbor takes on a whole new challenge.

- When you hear of someone in your church who just lost his or her job.
- When your next door neighbor needs help.
- When your neighbor who does not belong to your church loses his or her job.
- When your neighbor is sick.
- When your neighbor has car trouble.

Those can be challenging enough. How about these? Do you think of these people as your neighbor?

- When you hear of a temple or mosque defaced in this country, maybe in your city or town.
- When someone of another race or ethnicity needs your help.
- When an undocumented alien needs help.
- When you hear about the terrible persecution of Christians in other countries.
- The next time you hear about the terrible persecution of Muslims in your own city.
- When a Republican or Democrat or whoever you consider your political enemy needs help.
- When a Black man has stopped by the side of the road with obvious car trouble.
- When a White woman has stopped by the side of the road with obvious car trouble.

How can we love our neighbors as ourselves this way? Through the saving work of God, who brings us from death to life, who empowers us with the Holy Spirit, who enlivens in our hearts with a

Kingdom ethos that is reflective of Jesus the King, who loved us even when we were His enemies.

Notice one last thing in the parable. The Samaritan doesn't help everyone. He helps the person the Lord puts in front of him on the road. The King doesn't expect you to confront all injustice or to help every person or group of people who are in need. That is an impossible task and simply brings self-condemnation because we aren't helping everyone.[26]

The King calls us to love those who He puts in our path. It may be in helping an elderly neighbor with grocery shopping when he or she can't go to the grocery. It may be listening to an acquaintance share the pain of divorce or the loss of a loved one. It may happen in the form of giving financially to organizations and people who are doing good work in the areas that I carry a burden for but have no expertise or gifting. The point is that we have an open heart that is attuned to those in need and that is listening to the prompting of the Holy Spirit for those times when the King brings them our way on the road of our lives.

Now step back and look at all of the citizens of the Kingdom doing the same: loving their neighbor as themselves. This is the King's plan. It's not just a few helping many. It's not one person trying to help everyone. And it's not everyone loving their neighbor the same way. It's many helping and loving many. Loving them different ways. Each according to the opportunity and occasion the King presents them with. This is the genius of the Kingdom here on earth. The Kingdom becomes visible when all believers love our neighbors as ourselves.

26) However, as a matter of government policy, the Christian politician certainly needs to consider the way of the Good Samaritan when debating government assistance and relief programs. Likewise, regardless of political party, Christians, when considering legislation and government policies and elections, should have the mind of the Good Samaritan.

WHAT DOES LOVING YOUR NEIGHBOR LOOK LIKE?

The question becomes, what does that look like?

The scriptures are alive with how citizens in the Kingdom are to relate to others. For example, one of the best expressions of the Kingdom ethos is when Paul ends Romans this way. Take time to read this slowly. Savor its import and lovingkindness:

> Let love be genuine. Abhor what is evil; hold fast to what is good. Love one another with brotherly affection. Outdo one another in showing honor. Do not be slothful in zeal, be fervent in spirit, serve the Lord. Rejoice in hope, be patient in tribulation, be constant in prayer. Contribute to the needs of the saints and seek to show hospitality. Bless those who persecute you; bless and do not curse them. Rejoice with those who rejoice, weep with those who weep. Live in harmony with one another. Do not be haughty, but associate with the lowly. Never be wise in your own sight. Repay no one evil for evil, but give thought to do what is honorable in the sight of all. If possible, so far as it depends on you, live peaceably with all. Beloved, never avenge yourselves, but leave it to the wrath of God, for it is written, "Vengeance is mine, I will repay, says the Lord." To the contrary, "if your enemy is hungry, feed him; if he is thirsty, give him something to drink; for by so doing you will heap burning coals on his head." Do not be overcome by evil, but overcome evil with good. (Romans 12: 9-21)

This is a passage that the believer would do well to read and re-read every single day. Notice the many moral qualities brought out in the passage: Brotherly love, honoring others, generosity, hospitality, being empathetic towards others, humility towards all, kindness towards enemies. It encompasses attitudes and behavior not just towards other Christians but to all we meet. This is how citizens of the Kingdom of God treat others.

Kingdom ethos is likewise expounded by Jesus in the Sermon on the Mount (Matthew 5-7). He addresses:

- Those who are happy (blessed) in this life (Matthew 5: 2-12)
- The Kingdom ethos is apparent to the world (Matthew 5: 13-16)
- The Kingdom ethos is more than you think (Matthew 5: 17-20)
- The seriousness of anger (Matthew 5: 21-22)
- The need to quickly resolve offenses (Matthew 5: 23-26
- The seriousness of lust (Matthew 5: 27-30)
- The strict limits on divorce (Matthew 5: 31-32)
- The seriousness of taking oaths (Matthew 5: 33-37)
- Resist the urge for retaliation (Matthew 5: 38-42)
- Loving your enemies (Matthew 5: 43-48)
- The proper way to give to the needy (Matthew 6: 1-4)
- How to pray—The Lord's Prayer (Matthew 6: 5-13)
- Forgiving others (Matthew 6: 14-15)
- How to fast (Matthew 6: 16-18)
- Choosing heavenly treasure over worldly treasure (Matthew 6: 19-24)
- Why you shouldn't fall prey to anxiety (Matthew 6: 25-34)
- Warnings against judging others (Matthew 7: 1-6)
- The call to ask what you need from a loving God (Matthew 7: 7-11)
- The Golden Rule—do unto others as you would have them do unto you (Matthew 7: 12)
- The narrow gate into the Kingdom of God (Matthew 7: 13-14)
- Recognizing people by the fruit in their life (Matthew 7: 15-20)
- God must know you to be in the Kingdom of God (Matthew 7: 21-23)

- The necessity to build your life on hearing the King's words and doing them (Matthew 7: 24-27)

As is clear from just these two examples of scripture, a deep dive into the Kingdom ethos in terms of how we treat others would require volumes. Instead, let's look at just three more examples. And, interestingly, they come not from the New Testament but the Old Testament.

The prophet Micah prophesied around 700 B.C. It was a time that bore some similarities to our own. The kingdoms of Israel and Judah were experiencing a period of great economic prosperity and external strength against its enemies. Yet both were afflicted by a rising internal and spiritual decadence:

> While Israel and Judah appeared to be strong externally, an internal decay was sapping their strength and threatening to destroy the social fabric of these two kingdoms. A burgeoning wealthy class was becoming richer at the expense of the poorer classes ... But the internal sickness of Israel involved more than social wrongs. Canaanite religion also had extended its influence among some of the people. And while Micah attacked the idolatry that accompanied the acceptance of Canaanite worship, it was not this aspect of Israel's condition that he emphasized most. It was rather the social injustices of the ruling classes to which Micah gave the greatest attention.[27]

Sound familiar? Two thousand, seven hundred years later, the United States is the wealthiest country in the history of the world. And while many enjoy the prosperity of that wealth, there is a growing disparity between the wealthy and the poor, and many injustices abound.

27) *The Expositor's Bible Commentary*, Volume 7 (Zondervan Publishing, 1985) p. 395

In Micah 6:8, the Lord chastises the Israelites for the hypocrisy in their lives. They bring him abundant sacrifices while living lives that contradict what He has told them is good. He then tell them three things He requires of His people: "He has told you, O man, what is good; and what does the LORD require of you but to *do justice, and to love kindness, and to walk humbly with your God?*" (Micah 6:8, emphasis added).

Do justice. Love kindness. Walk humbly. That is Kingdom ethos.

The King isn't interested in a group of Kingdom citizens who love going to church but then forget what goodness lived the rest of the week looks like. He has created a Kingdom that is alive with His goodness. And it looks like something in particular. Let's examine each of these three qualities more closely.

DO JUSTICE

Christians should be the most active and engaged people in the world when it comes to justice. Because the King is just and calls us to do justice. And doing justice is a way of loving your neighbor.

In the United States, the topic of justice has freshly erupted in the national consciousness. Social justice, structural racism, Black Lives Matter, Critical Race Theory—it has become a season of white hot argument, protest, confrontation, and even violence and death. Likewise, we see justice issues have come to the fore in other countries around the world, be they racial or ethnic injustice, treatment of immigrants who are fleeing desperate conditions of their home country, struggles against totalitarianism, or exploitation of the poor.

While the issue of justice has burst forth in a new way for many, the Christian should not have been unprepared for the conversation because justice has been one of the elements of a Kingdom ethos since the beginning when God asked Adam what he had done with the forbidden fruit. Christians who don't have a good understanding of justice or who aren't active with justice have been asleep at the wheel. Tim Keller makes this point:

> In the Bible Christians have an ancient, rich, strong, comprehensive, complex, and attractive understanding of justice. Biblical justice differs in significant ways from all the secular alternatives, without ignoring the concerns of any of them. Yet Christians know little about biblical justice, despite its prominence in the Scriptures. This ignorance is having two effects. First, large swaths of the church still do not see "doing justice" as part of their calling as individual believers. Second, many younger Christians, recognizing this failure of the church and wanting to rectify things, are taking up one or another of the secular approaches to justice, which introduces distortions into their practice and lives.[28]

The Kingdom ethos is to "do justice." It is an imperative. The Christian must actively live a life of justice.

Justice can be simply defined as the application of what is right and fair equitably among people. Put another way, justice is people treating other people rightly and fairly by an agreed upon set of ethical or moral standards.

Micah gives an example: "Shall I acquit the man with wicked scales and with a bag of deceitful weights? Your rich men are full of violence; your inhabitants speak lies, and their tongue is deceitful

28) Tim Keller, "A Biblical Critique of Social Justice and Critical Theory", Life in the Gospel, August 2020, https://quarterly.gospelinlife.com/a-biblical-critique-of-secular-justice-and-critical-theory/

in their mouth" (Micah 6: 11-12). In this case, lying and deceit in business is not just unethical, it is unjust. A modern example could be redlining practiced by banks when determining who would get a mortgage or insurance and the loan or rate was based on the racial makeup of the community. A Black person who would otherwise be eligible for a mortgage would be denied the loan because of their race. That's injustice.

Biblical Justice

The trick is that justice can mean something very different to different people depending on where you start. To a Marxist, justice has its own meaning. Biblical justice has a particular meaning and it is rooted in the fact that God is just: "Justice is a communicable attribute of God, manifesting his holiness. The biblical words thus translated, *sedaqa*, *sedaq*, and *dikaiosyne* are also translated 'righteousness'".[29]

So to understand biblical justice, we start with the fact that God Himself is righteous and just. Thus, the Kingdom ethos of justice proceeds foundationally from God. And what God declares to be right and just sets the standard for knowing if the way a person or people are treated is just or unjust.

Here we see the connection with the second great command, love your neighbor as yourself. Love for your neighbor necessitates treating your neighbor justly. This proposition has both a negative and positive implication. One cannot engage in criminal activity and love their neighbor. And when we make sure that a person of color has the same rights as a White person that is justice and love.

Once our basic understanding of biblical justice is established, then we can look to various qualities attached to justice.

29) *Evangelical Dictionary of Theology*, Walter Elwell, Ed., (Baker Book House, 1984) p. 593

Here's just one example of how to approach justice biblically. It's not the only way. It's not a comprehensive treatment. But it is very different than starting from a secular point of view. In an article titled, "Justice in the Bible,"[30] Tim Keller outlines four facets of biblical justice:

1. It is equitable, that is everyone must be treated equally and with dignity (Leviticus 19:15 and Deuteronomy 16:19).

2. It calls for generous stewardship of God's wealth (1 Chronicles 29:14; 1 Corinthians 4:7, and Luke 16:1-16).

3. The individual shares in a corporate responsibility to see justice done: (Daniel 9. 2 Samuel 21, Joshua 7, Numbers 16, 1 Samuel 15:2. and Deuteronomy 23:3-8).

4. We must have special concern for the poor and the marginalized (Psalm 41:1, Proverbs 29:7, Deuteronomy 24:17, 19)

What this means is that Christians have both a personal and corporate responsibility to do justice. It means personal behavior. It means personal advocacy. It also means aligning corporately with justice issues in the world.

Doing Justice Today

This book is about big questions. Here's an important question: "Are you doing justice?" In other words, in living out a Kingdom ethos of justice, our lives should be a light on the hill when it comes to justice. Our lives relative to justice should be noticed by others. The follow-up question becomes: "What can you point to that shows you to be gripped by doing justice?"

What does it look like? It's writing your government representatives. It means speaking up and not being silent when silence con-

30) Tim Keller, "Justice in the Bible", Life in the Gospel, September 2020, https://quarterly. gospelinlife.com/justice-in-the-bible/

dones injustice. It means sometimes getting out and protesting. It means donating your money to just causes. It may mean working in and with organizations that are pursuing biblical justice. It means voting with biblical justice in the forefront for who you vote for. Or who you do not vote for. It may mean losing your job, your home, your education because you don't support injustice in the country you live in. These are just a few examples of doing justice.

Examples of Biblical Justice

For example:

- Biblical justice argues for a pro-life position for the unborn. All life is God-given. God creates us and knits us in the womb. And there is no weaker life in the world that an unborn child. Shall we tell God to stop creating that life in the mother's womb? Shall we destroy what God is making in His image and likeness?
- Biblical justice means that Black lives do, in fact, matter. We are all created in Gods image and Blacks have suffered injustices and still suffer from explicit racism and less explicit racial prejudice.
- Biblical justice also means that injustice towards poor Whites and Hispanics and Asian Americans also matter. Rather than fixate on a slogan, let's remember God's call to love our neighbor, which means that we speak out against injustice whatever the race or ethnicity.
- Biblical justice means we advocate against human trafficking and sexual slavery, which is rampant even in a country like the United States.
- Biblical justice means we support efforts against religious perse-cution in the United States and abroad.
- Biblical justice argues for a humane and generous treatment of un-documented aliens. We are told, "Thus says the LORD: Do justice

and righteousness, and deliver from the hand of the oppressor him who has been robbed. And do no wrong or violence to the resident alien, the fatherless, and the widow, nor shed innocent blood in this place." (Jeremiah 22:3) The scriptures make no distinction about the legal status of the alien.

- On the other hand, biblical justice supports the laws of the land as long as they don't contravene the King's justice. So we should recognize that illegal entry into the country is wrong and that the government has the right to enforce those laws against it.

- We have to think through the fact that injustice can become systemic, where the individual sins of many becomes so widespread that it infects parts of our society, be it certain police departments, certain educational systems, or certain health systems. In this regard, we refer to the idea of unequal scales such as Proverbs 23:3: "Unequal weights are an abomination to the LORD, and false scales are not good." So, for example, when school systems are based primarily or substantially on real estate taxes, that necessarily means that poor areas in a state will always have less funding than rich areas in that state. The scales are unequal. And poor children, who are often but not entirely minority children, are disadvantaged in their education in the United States.

- On the other hand, biblical justice demands that we obey those in authority over us, including the police and our government. As Paul writes in Romans 13: 1-2: "Let every person be subject to the governing authorities. For there is no authority except from God, and those that exist have been instituted by God. Therefore whoever resists the authorities resists what God has appointed, and those who resist will incur judgment." There is no room for violence and insurrection against the God given authorities in the land.

The point is that how we approach justice must begin with the Kingdom's ethos, its moral and ethical commands and principles, applied with wisdom and humility, led by the Spirit.

Biblical Justice Is Not the Property of a Political Party

Thinking that one political party speaks for biblical justice and one does not is overly simplistic and ultimately prevents you from doing justice biblically. What matters is that each of us is doing justice. Before the King, not a party.

In fact, doing biblical justice will likely put you at odds with any particular political party. Tim Keller puts it this way:

> For example, following both the Bible and the early church, Christians should be committed to racial justice and the poor, but also to the understanding that sex is only for marriage and for nurturing family. One of those views seems liberal and the other looks oppressively conservative. The historical Christian positions on social issues do not fit into contemporary political alignments.[31]

The Yes But … Temptation

While the Kingdom ethos on justice should be operative in us all the time, too often we have reasons for not "doing justice." I call this the "Yes, but.." subversion of justice. We find loopholes, we have excuses, we don't want to put the time into thinking an issue through. We point out the injustice or ethical failings by others. We fail to think biblically and instead adopt political arguments and ideologies. Or we unthinkingly adopt the views of justice by other worldviews.

---

31) Tim Keller, "How Do Christians Fit Into the Two-Party System? They Don't", *The New York Times*, September 29, 2018

In the Kingdom of God, the Christian doesn't find reasons to avoid doing justice. Instead, the Christian is aware that the King is a just King and He delights in His people knowing and doing what is right and good to others. And His delight in what is right and fair should be our delight. That way, our initial response is not arguing against action; instead we are motivated by the desire to see justice flow like a river. We don't cherry pick our issues. All of life—personal and corporate—is weighed on the scales of justice, fairness, and righteousness.

Doing biblical justice changes everything.

LOVE KINDNESS

The King also requires us to love kindness …

Kindness is underrated in the pantheon of character qualities. It's not one of those power qualities like love or wisdom or peace. And that, I think, is why it is one of the three things the Lord calls out in Micah. Kindness changes everything.

Kindness is the active, gracious orientation of goodness and generosity towards others, including those who don't deserve it. It's active. Kindness is doing good or being generous or speaking encouragingly. It is benevolent—it is born out of a desire for the good of your neighbor. It is gracious because it isn't earned, it is freely given without any expectation of receiving anything in return.

Like any other ethical qualities, anyone in the world can be kind. But Kingdom kindness is a fruit of the Spirit meaning it is birthed by and sustained by the Holy Spirit. And it is an ongoing quality; we don't just do kind things, we are a kind people. It is in our Kingdom constitution to be kind. Paul writes in Ephesians 4 that we are to keep being continually being filled by the Spirit, which means that Kingdom kindness is like a constantly flowing spring from God though us.

The command is not to just be kind but to love being kind. In the Kingdom of God, the Kingdom ethos loves to freely and willingly show kindness to others. It includes generosity, hospitality, and encouragement. It's simply the way we are made to be in the Kingdom. And we love being that way.

So many of the actions Paul wrote about in the passage cited above from Romans 12 are acts of kindness:

- Love one another with brotherly affection.
- Outdo one another in showing honor.
- Contribute to the needs of the saints and seek to show hospitality.
- Bless those who persecute you; bless and do not curse them.
- Rejoice with those who rejoice, weep with those who weep.
- Live in harmony with one another.
- Repay no one evil for evil, but give thought to do what is honorable in the sight of all.
- If possible, so far as it depends on you, live peaceably with all.
- If your enemy is hungry, feed him; if he is thirsty, give him something to drink.

We are tempted to think that the best way to share the gospel is being well versed in the gospel and in apologetics so we can answer every question a non-Christian has. On the contrary, while we must be able to give a reason for the hope that is in us, it is kindness that more often wins the day. Steven Whitmer relates the following story:

> In her memoir about the journey from being a committed lesbian to a committed Christian, Rosaria Butterfield says that, as a non-Christian, her impression of evangelical Christians was that they were poor thinkers, judgmental, scornful, and afraid of diversity. After publishing a critique of an evangelical Christian group in her local newspaper, she received an enormous

volume of polarized responses. Placing an empty box in each corner of her desk, she sorted hate mail into one and fan mail into the other.

Then she received a two-page response from a local pastor. "It was a kind and inquiring letter," she says. It had a warmth and civility to it, in addition to its probing questions. She couldn't figure out which box to put the letter in, so it sat on her desk for seven days. "It was the kindest letter of opposition that I had ever received." Its tone demonstrated that the writer wasn't against her.

Eventually, she contacted the pastor and became friends with him and his wife. "They talked with me in a way that didn't make me feel erased." Their friendship was an important part of her journey to faith.[32]

Kingdom kindness is not reserved for our friends or fellow Christians. It is color-blind, ethnicity-blind, and gender-blind. It changes everything.

WALK HUMBLY

When we talk about a great and mighty King, the King of kings, when we talk about the eternal, splendid kingdom of kingdoms, when we think of saints and angels populating this Kingdom, of all the ways of living that we would expect the King to require of us, what comes to mind first? Courage? Power? Righteousness? Love?

Nope. Humility. We are to walk humbly. That's at the top of God's list. Consider how the scriptures speak of humility and the

---

32) Stephen Witmer, "Kindness Changes Everything", September 4, 2016, Desiring God Ministries, https://www.desiringgod.org/articles/kindness-changes-everything

humble person: "I therefore, a prisoner for the Lord, *urge you to walk in a manner worthy of the calling to which you have been called, with all humility and gentleness,* with patience, bearing with one another in love, eager to maintain the unity of the Spirit in the bond of peace" (Ephesians 4: 1-3, emphasis added).

The King calls us to walk this way. It elevates our lives as citizens. It is the way in which we live worthy lives before the King.

There are no separate classes inside the Kingdom. We are all one and it is only the King that matters:

Here there is not Greek and Jew, circumcised and uncircumcised, barbarian, Scythian, slave, free; but Christ is all, and in all. *Put on then*, as God's chosen ones, holy and beloved, compassionate hearts, kindness, *humility*, meekness, and patience, bearing with one another and, if one has a complaint against another, forgiving each other; as the Lord has forgiven you, so you also must forgive (Colossians 3:11-13, emphasis added).

In fact, it is how we are to live with one another not just in the Kingdom but also towards those not in the Kingdom.

Humility is defined as a modest or low view of one's own importance. It conveys the idea that we do not exalt ourselves, rather, we take a low view of our importance and significance. Jonathan Edwards explains Christian humility this way:

A truly humble man is sensible of his natural distance from God; of his dependence on Him; of the insufficiency of his own power and wisdom; and that it is by God's power that he is upheld and provided for, and that he needs God's wisdom to lead and guide him, and His might to enable him to do what he ought to do for Him.[33]

It is not self-loathing. It is not self-hatred. For the citizen of the Kingdom of God, humility doesn't trash the God given graces in self-abnegation. Instead, it is a position of oneself relative to others believing we are no greater or better or of more value, and, most significantly, that the King is the only one worthy of importance and value and exaltation.

It is important to understand how the King views pride, the opposite of humility: "Everyone who is arrogant in heart is an abomination to the LORD; be assured, he will not go unpunished" (Proverbs 16:5). Pride is an abomination. Not just wrong or bad. An abomination. Something that causes disgust and hatred. God is disgusted by pride.

Why does the King want us to walk humbly and what does it accomplish? Humility accomplishes several things in the Kingdom of God.

Humility Lets Us Live Rightly Before the King

First, humility positions us to live rightly before the King. To live out a Kingdom ethos, the King must always be before us. And when we rightly apprehend the King, it humbles us. He is the righteous one, not us. He is the loving one, not us. He is the wise one, not us. He is the giver of life, not us. The humble citizen is amazed at the grace of God that we might stand in the King's presence, serve the King, be loved by the King. Just as we are amazed at the grace that saves us, we are amazed and humbled at the privilege to live before and serve the King.

33) Jonathan Edwards, *Charity and Its Fruits*, Edited by Tryon Edwards (James Nesbit & Co, 1852) p. 133

Humility is the Catalyst for the Rest of the Kingdom Ethos

Second, humility is the catalyst for the Kingdom ethos: "Clothe yourselves, all of you, with *humility* toward one another, for "God opposes the proud but gives grace to the humble." (I Peter 5:5, emphasis added).

It is the humble person who is rightly positioned to receive the full measure of the King's grace, in this case His unmerited enabling power, to live a life pleasing to the King and graciously towards others.

Likewise, it is the humble person who is in a position to be guided by the King in what is right: "He leads the humble in what is right, and teaches the humble his way" (Psalm 25:9).

In other words, all other qualities that constitute the Kingdom ethos come only through a humble disposition. Think of it. How can we be loving, just, generous, forgiving, kind, in a genuine, Christ-like manner if we aren't humble first? To the extent that we let our pride and vanity and self-importance reign in our heart, we cannot be kind and gentle and loving and generous and forgiving. Conversely, the more humble we become, the more all other qualities become possible. Humility makes a way for true Kingdom habits, thoughts and actions.

Humility Displays the Kingdom of God to Non-Christians

Finally, humility displays the Kingdom of God to non-Christians like no other moral quality other than love.

American culture has an odd relationship with humility. On one hand, it is respected in a certain way. "He/She was humble, wasn't he/she?" Respected, but not encouraged to be emulated.

Humility is typically not held up as a positive means for advancement, promotion, or success. It is often mistaken for weakness, timidity, or a lack of initiative. And in this increasingly strident age when the loudest voices, the bullying voices, the interrupting voices, the intolerant voices are the voices that often carry the day. The humble man and woman are not the model for American politics, business, sports, or even education.

So when the citizen of the Kingdom of God lives humbly—be it politics, business, sports, education, etc.—it stands out. It forces those who see it, who are the objects of a humble word or deed, to process it. Jesus says: "You are the light of the world. A city set on a hill cannot be hidden. Nor do people light a lamp and put it under a basket, but on a stand, and it gives light to all in the house" (Matthew 5: 13-14).

He is telling us that the Kingdom ethos, including our Spirit given humility, is that light. We aren't a literal light. It is the quality and character of our life—manifested in our words and deeds and actions and habits—that causes our life to shine out before a world increasingly enveloped in darkness.

Walking humbly changes the world.

CONCLUSION

Being in the Kingdom of God means being changed in how we treat others, think about others, speak to others, and help others.

It is more than just a list of rules or maxims. It is a certain kind of person. And while we won't make a celebrity list by the way we live, it will be a life that is noticed by those around us. Some will be drawn to that kind of life. Others will mock it. Mock you.

More importantly, it will be a life that the King watches, enables, and delights in because it is the way He was when He walked this Earth. In His life on Earth, Jesus embodied this idea of doing justice, loving kindness, and walking humbly.

Jesus's life was loving others, including His enemies. Jesus's life was marked by compassion for the poor, the weak, and the helpless.

His life was a life of loved lived out towards the marginal and the unclean. He never excused sin but He loved those who were trapped by their sin. He didn't live for the approval of others or for some kind of worldly acclaim. He always had His calling from the Father in mind. And, in the end, He died for those who rejected Him.

The Kingdom of God and the King call us to live radically different lives towards others from what the world offers. It changes everything.

9

The Ethos of the Kingdom— Our Inward Life

THUS FAR, WE'VE SEEN HOW the Kingdom ethos governs how we relate to the King and to others. But a Kingdom ethos also means an inward orientation, a way of being. It is that effect on our own heart and mind and soul. It governs our emotions and our dispositions and our attitudes irrespective of others or external conditions. Paul puts it this way: "For the kingdom of God is not a matter of eating and drinking, but of righteousness, peace and joy in the Holy Spirit" (Romans 14:17). This is the internal presence of the Kingdom.

Many people, including Christians, live in such a way that their happiness is found in the pursuit of pleasure. Good food, good drink, the right clothes, bucket list vacations and adventures, exciting new technologies, the right house, the right neighborhood—all these external sources of pleasure and enjoyment become the basis for our happiness and contentment.

But the Kingdom ethos speaks of an inward way of life. In the Kingdom, there is a way to just be. It isn't about what we do or say or have or don't have. It's how we live inside ourselves. And when we not only grasp this but live in the good of it, it changes our lives.

115

Let's look at each of these elements from Romans 14 as an illustration of this inner dimension of the Kingdom ethos.

RIGHTEOUSNESS

Righteousness is both an action and an attitude. For example, practically speaking, it means that our conscience, attitude, and actions towards God and others cannot entertain hate and evil. As George Eldon Ladd says: "Kingdom righteousness demands that I have no evil in my heart towards my fellow man."[34] The heart. There is no room for lying, slander, hatred, anger, or coarse speech because they violate the Kingdom ethos. And they come from within.

But righteousness isn't just a matter of not doing something. It is, primarily, the love and doing of what is good and right and true. So Paul can call on us: "Finally, brothers and sisters, whatever is true, whatever is noble, whatever is right, whatever is pure, whatever is lovely, whatever is admirable—if anything is excellent or praiseworthy—think about such things" (Philippians 4:8).

Notice that Paul doesn't say to do something. He calls us to "think about such things." It is an internal condition first. Righteousness begins in the heart and mind. It is a disposition that delights in what is good and true and noble and pure and lovely. Action and speech will follow but first and foremost, righteousness is a condition of the heart. That is how the Kingdom ethos works.

PEACE

My youngest daughter used to have a very stressful and demanding job, physically and emotionally. From time to time, she would come spend the weekend with us, at the house where she had lived for

---

34) George Eldon Ladd, *Ibid*, p. 83

many years. We live in a very quiet, beautiful, little town. One square mile large. However, it is surrounded by major roadways, the University of Maryland, a shopping center, and not entirely the safest surroundings … you get the picture. It was an unpeaceful world outside our peaceful little town. When my daughter would enter our town, there was a sign with the words "Traffic Calming" announcing the speedbumps that forced you to slow down. When she saw that sign, she could feel a change come over her. The stress of her life started to ease. The noise of the outside world started to recede as she slowly drove through the tree-lined residential streets towards our house. She would drive up and park and come inside. Home. She was home. And a joyful, calm peace settled over her.

We often shortchange the idea of peace, thinking of it as no more than the absence of war or conflict. But biblical peace, also called shalom, is far richer than that. It's not just the absence of strife and conflict but the positive sense of harmony, of everything being the way it should be. Cornelius Plantinga describes biblical peace this way:

> In the Bible, shalom means universal flourishing, wholeness and delight—a rich state of affairs in which natural needs are satisfied and natural gifts fruitfully employed, a state of affairs that inspires joyful wonder as its Creator and Savior opens doors and welcomes the creatures in whom he delights. Shalom, in other words, is the way things ought to be.[35]

Peace. The way things ought to be. "Peace I give to you," says Jesus. No longer objects of God's wrath but beloved children of God. No lon-

35) Cornelius Plantinga, *Not the Way It's Supposed to Be: A Breviary of Sin* (Eerdmans Publishing, 1996) p.10

ger slaves to sin but loving servants of the great King of the Kingdom of God. No longer trying to find and desperately hold onto a peace that is no peace, be it from a life of affluence or the approval of others.

It is a peace that is given by grace alone, not earned. A peace in which we can be still and know that He is God. A peace that dwells in us and stays with us. A peace that passes understanding and that enables us to bear up under the trials of this world. Peace. The way it ought to be.

The shalom peace spoken of in scripture anchors us internally and lets us experience peace with God. And then, along with righteousness, joy, and love, peace guides us in our interactions with others.

JOY

The word "joy" comes from the Greek word *chara*, which describes a feeling of inner gladness, delight or rejoicing. Joy is a feeling of inner gladness, delight or rejoicing. It is a deep seated pleasure. Joy isn't a superficial happiness. It's more settled. There is a deep, soul-satisfying pleasure. Let me give you an example.

My four children are all grown now. And I love and treasure them all. In fact, there are now four "grand treasures," as we refer to our grandchildren. But after all this time, I can still remember that moment when my first born, my son, was born. After a long and challenging delivery, there he was. The nurse brought him to me all swaddled and put him in my arms. And he looked right into my eyes. For a minute, it was just him and me; the rest of the world seemed to simply fade away. I know the experts say that newborns can't smile, and their brains aren't wired to consciously connect. But when he looked into my eyes … well, it was a connecting moment. We just looked at each other. It was just more than happiness. What I felt was deep, deep pleasure—joy.

To be sure, joy is something any person can experience. You don't have to be a Christian. But in the Kingdom of God, joy comes from God. There is a joy that is settled and unshakeable. A deep-seated pleasure in God. And a deep-seated pleasure from God.

Let that sink in. In a world of sadness, depression, hopelessness, anger, and frustration, there is joy in the Kingdom. Don't be mistaken. In this world, we will experience great sadnesses. We will mourn. Many of us will go through seasons of depression and loss. But for the citizen of the Kingdom of God, the promise is that there is joy. Unfettered deep pleasure in God and from God.

IN THE HOLY SPIRIT

The last phrase in the passage is the key: "The Kingdom of God is a matter of righteousness, peace, and joy *in the Holy Spirit*" (emphasis added).

The empowering presence of the Holy Spirit is a hallmark of the Kingdom. As the Apostle Paul says in 1 Corinthians 4: 20: "For the kingdom of God does not consist in talk but in power." The Holy Spirit animates the Kingdom of God and everyone in it in a powerful way. This includes natural and supernatural gifts and qualities. And it is by the power of the Holy Spirit that these three qualities—righteousness, peace, and joy—are communicated and sustained in the spirit of every believer.

The righteousness, peace, and joy that we have in the Kingdom of God is God originated and God sustained:

> Romans 5:17 says: "For if, because of one man's trespass, death reigned through that one man, much more will those who receive the abundance of grace and *the free gift of righteousness reign in life through the one man Jesus Christ*" (emphasis added).

119

John 14:17 says: "Peace I leave with you; *my peace I give to you.* Not as the world gives do I give to you. Let not your hearts be troubled, neither let them be afraid" (emphasis added).

In Galatians 5: 22, we read: But the fruit of the Spirit is love, *joy*, peace, patience, kindness, goodness, faithfulness, gentleness, self-control; against such things there is no law" (emphasis added).

Can non-Christians experience peace and joy and righteousness? Of course. But this passage in Romans speaks of the experience of these qualities "in the Holy Spirit." And that is a critical distinction.

In the case of the Christian, these things don't depend on external circumstances. They don't depend on others. They don't depend even on us. Righteousness, joy and peace come from God and are sustained in us by God the power of the Holy Spirit. This is something very different from what non-Christians experience.

Think about this. There are joys in this life that are big and meaningful. But they can be lost. They can ebb and flow. The joy of marriage can be extinguished by divorce or simply by growing apart. The peace of a home can be lost by time and distance. The righteousness of doing right can be overturned by lies, deceptions, selfishness and greed. But righteousness, peace, and joy in the Holy Spirit aren't subject to such conditions. Our union in Christ is not conditioned on human effort or temporal conditions. It is conditioned on the unchanging, all-powerful God. It's unshakeable. That's a different kind of internal human condition. And it is part of our life in the Kingdom of God.

PUT IT ALL TOGETHER

My wife loves art. And when she sees a picture, she studies it exhaustively. Sometimes, she may spend thirty or forty minutes on a single picture. She looks up close at the coloring, the shadowing, the spacing, the lines, the texture, and the brush strokes. She will even look at the frame for a long time. All the components of the picture. (Meanwhile, I am at the café enjoying the afternoon sun.) But then she steps back and looks at the picture as a whole. She sees how it all comes together and stands in admiration at what the artist has created.

While it is beneficial to reflect on each of these qualities—righteousness, joy, and peace—it's important to see them combined in our hearts. Step back and try to imagine a person whose nature is composed of these qualities. It is a particular kind of person. This is the internal condition of the citizen of the Kingdom. It's how the King means for us to be. We have within us, right now, this incredible, unmatched gift from the King.

One of the great questions of life is, "Who am I?" Instead of listening to the world tell you that you are nothing more than another temporary living organism with a life span of seventy or eighty years, instead of listening to others define you by your color or ethnicity or nationality, instead of you telling yourself that you are permanently wounded or a champion in life or whatever, listen to the King. You are His beloved child/servant to whom He has sent the Holy Spirit that you might be a person whose identity and constitution is rooted in righteousness, joy, and peace. And isn't that a wonderful thing?

WHY IS THIS SO HARD?—EXPATS VS. CITIZENS

If you are like me, this all sounds so good; so why does it seem so elusive at times? I know how I am supposed to live but so often, I do the opposite.

There are several reasons why we stumble as citizens—indwelling sin (the flesh) and the Devil are two reasons—but let me add one more reason why we make it so hard on ourselves.

There are people who are citizens of one country but who live in another. They stay in the foreign country sometimes for a few years, sometimes for the rest of their lives. They aren't tourists. In their case, they prefer the foreign country over their native land, not enough to become a citizen of the other country but enough to immerse themselves in the culture of that country. Whether for politics or the people or the way of life or simply as an escape, they disconnect from their country of origin and make their home in another country. Citizens of one country making their home in another. Not really a citizen of either country.

For example, in the 1920's, a number of American writers and artists left the United States and moved to Europe, Paris in particular for many. These included Ernest Hemingway, F. Scott Fitzgerald, and Ezra Pound. They left for various reasons: disaffected by the politics, policies, and wealth of the United States, disillusioned about the carnage of World War I, etc. Gertrude Stein, a writer of that age, called them the "lost generation." The word we use for people like this is expatriates or expats.

I would argue that there is something called "expat Christians." They have settled outside the Kingdom of God. They have adopted the customs and preferences and ways of thinking of this world over the Kingdom. They would never say it out loud but they are content to not just be in the world, but be part of it.

Expat Christians are those who barely make it in because of the poor foundation of their faith and life. As Paul describes them, "If the work that anyone has built on the foundation survives, he will receive a reward. If anyone's work is burned up, he will suffer loss, though he himself will be saved, but only as through fire" (1 Corinthians 3: 14-15). The expat believer will come through scorched by fire with little or nothing to show for his or her life. In Revelation 2 and 3, we read of the Lord's warning to churches that had expat Christians among them: In Ephesus they had abandoned the love they had at first; in Pergamum they had allowed false teachings to take root; in Thyatira they were guilty of sexual immortality and idolatry; in Sardis they had a reputation for being alive but were dead; in Laodicea they were neither hot nor cold, they were lukewarm because of their wealth. Why? Maybe they became disillusioned by what they saw in the church. Or they fell prey to the temptations of the world. But fundamentally, they didn't embrace the supremacy of Kingdom life.

The same holds true today. Like expats living in other countries, Christian expats become like the world they live in. They pick up its speech, its dress, its food, its way of thinking, and its pleasures. They talk like the world does, they joke like the world does, they do politics like the world does, and they even do religion like the world does. Christian expats live like Kingdom citizens in name only. In immersing themselves in the world they live in, they become like the world. There is little that distinguishes them. The life and power of the Kingdom of God resides in them like an inert force. They become the "lost generation" of the Kingdom of God.

By all standards, the claims of life in the Kingdom of God are superior to anything offered in this life. In fact, however, too many Christians are living happily in the dregs of this life when life in the Kingdom is so much better. The famous quote from C.S. Lewis sums it up beautifully:

> If we consider the unblushing promises of reward and the staggering nature of the rewards promised in the Gospels, it would seem that Our Lord finds our desires not too strong, but too weak. We are half-hearted creatures, fooling about with drink and sex and ambition when infinite joy is offered us, like an

ignorant child who wants to go on making mud pies in a slum because he cannot imagine what is meant by the offer of a holiday at the sea. We are far too easily pleased.[36]

The "rewards promised in the Gospels" aren't simply salvation from our sins. It is life with God, with the King in the Kingdom of God.

Instead of living as expats in this world, Jesus, our King, wants us to live life-fulfilling lives as citizens of the Kingdom. For there is a way to live, an ethos, if you will, that isn't about legalistic commands but speaks to a Kingdom culture that elevates us out of the mud and into the glorious atmosphere of the great King and His Kingdom.

CONCLUSION AND A REALITY CHECK

In reading all this, it may sound like being a citizen in the Kingdom of God is supposed to be a walk in the park. But we know this isn't the case. One of the great appeals of the Christian faith is that it is realistic about life.

There are trials and temptation. There are seasons of plenty and season of want. There are highs and lows. There is suffering.

With regards to suffering, D.A. Carson says:

All we have to do is live long enough and we will suffer. Our loved ones will die; we ourselves will be afflicted with some diseases or other. Midlife often brings its own pressures—disappointments, sense of failure, decreasing physical strength, infidelity. Parents frequently go through enormous heartache in rearing their children.[37]

36) C.S Lewis, *The Weight of Glory and Other Addresses* (MacMillan Publishers, 1980) p. 26
37) D.A. Carson, *How Long O Lord?* (Baker Book House, 1990) p. 16

He goes on to say:

Despite the best efforts of the proponents of the health and wealth gospel, the fact is that Christians get wrinkled and old. They contract cancer and heart disease, become deaf and blind, and eventually die. In many parts of the world, Christians have to face the blight of famine, the scourge of war, the subtle coercion of corruption.[38]

Suffering, loss, grief, and deprivation are all part of living in this world. But the Kingdom of God takes that into account. It does not turn a blind eye to it. There is no effort to pretend that it doesn't happen to believers. Quite the contrary. The Kingdom of God gives us a practical theology on suffering and trials and failures and loss. Paul writes of the fact of suffering in 2 Corinthians 1:

Blessed be the God and Father of our Lord Jesus Christ, the Father of mercies and God of all comfort, who comforts us in all our affliction, so that we may be able to comfort those who are in any affliction, with the comfort with which we ourselves are comforted by God. For as we share abundantly in Christ's sufferings, so through Christ we share abundantly in comfort too. If we are afflicted, it is for your comfort and salvation; and if we are comforted, it is for your comfort, which you experience when you patiently endure the same sufferings that we suffer. Our hope for you is unshaken, for we know that as you share in our sufferings, you will also share in our comfort (2 Corinthians 1: 3-7).

38) D.A. Carson, *Ibid*, p. 69

Paul not only acknowledges that suffering will come to us but gives us a beautiful picture of how it should happen in the Kingdom of God. We suffer and others comfort us. Others suffer and we comfort them. Here is the call to love our neighbor as ourselves in a beautiful form.

Living as a citizen of the Kingdom certainly takes effort. But it is a God-enabled effort. It's grace. Not the grace that saves you but the grace, the unmerited provision of ability, to live the way the King wants you to live in the Kingdom of God.

And that is so important to understand. It is not an effort you undertake on your own. The King Himself wants you to live this way. He is for you in every moment and through the Holy Spirit strengthens you, changes your heart and thinking, and gives you the grace to do it.

It changes everything.

Conclusion

THIS BOOK STARTED WITH A profound and eternally significant question that requires an answer: What is the Kingdom of God and why does it matter?

In Chapter 2, we offered this definition of the Kingdom of God:

The Kingdom of God is the loving, righteous, wise, and just rule and reign of Jesus Christ, the King, over a realm that includes all believers and angels. It was foretold and foreshadowed in the Old Testament and inaugurated by Jesus's ascension to heaven after His resurrection. It is now in force fully in heaven, while here on earth it is present in and through all true believers through the agency of the Holy Spirit. It expresses the glorious qualities of the King, which is the basis for the ethos for all behavior in the Kingdom. Jesus patiently waits for the completion of the gospel to fill the final roll of citizenry of the Kingdom, at which time He shall complete His rule over all of creation by returning to earth and creating a new heaven and new earth where He will dwell with His people.

Why does it matter? We've seen that it was the reason for which

Jesus came to Earth. It was the centerpiece of his preaching and his disciples made it part of the gospel proclamation. The Kingdom was and is His purpose and passion and it should be ours. It calls us to a particular way of life—in relationship to the King, in relationship to others, and internally in our own hearts. It calls us to a Kingdom-centered life, which radically changes how we live life.

The King does not let you have one foot in the Kingdom and one foot out. Either have a passion and plunge deeper into the Kingdom or stay outside the Kingdom, fooled into thinking that being lukewarm or that accommodation with the world and its values and pleasures is acceptable to the King. Be an embassy, not an expat.

So why is it so hard to be passionate about the Kingdom? One reason is why I wrote this book: the Kingdom of God has not had the prominence in sermons and teachings and books that it should have. Pastors and writers have done a wonderful job proclaiming the gospel of the cross. The same can't be said of the gospel of the Kingdom. The church is too ignorant of Jesus's great passion.

Another reason for not being passionate about the Kingdom is that we can't literally see the Kingdom in this world. What do you see when you look at your life and the world around you? What do you see and think and feel when you wake up in the morning and read the newspaper or listen to the news or read your social media feeds? What do you see when you go to work? When you go shopping? When you go to school? Do you see the Kingdom of God? It's not "there," is it? It's not like seeing and knowing where your country is. Or the state you live in. Or even your neighborhood or home. It's not a place of work. There is no physical location. There are no boundaries. Not seeing it causes you to see your life and others the wrong way.

If this idea of seeing the invisible is difficult to imagine, consider that the most important things in life are invisible. What do you need more than anything in life? Oxygen. You can't see it. But you can't live more than a few minutes without it. And how about love? You can't see love. You can see its outworking, its effects, and its demonstration. But you can't see love. And yet, what is life without love? Lastly, how about salvation? Do you "see" your salvation? Of course not. You receive it by faith. You experience it, but you can't point to salvation like you would to a book or a cross or a building.

Likewise the Kingdom of God. It is invisible, yet it's there, and it is vitally important to "see" it. You are in it. And it is in you. And it is there in the hearts of all other believers in the world. And it's in heaven too.

Sounds good, doesn't it? But how does the Kingdom occupy the place in our hearts and minds and life the way the King wants it to? Jerry Bridges, a writer and teacher, taught that in order for us to live a life more fully in accordance with the gospel, we should preach the gospel to ourselves every day. Not because we need to be saved again but to remember the basic truths of our salvation and to regularly draw back closer to the saving work of Jesus. He understood that we drift. We forget. We "leak" the gospel. And so we preach the gospel to ourselves daily lest we drift from the blessings and calling of our great salvation.

We should do the same with the Kingdom of God. We need to daily reaffirm that we are citizens of the Kingdom. We should daily remind ourselves that we were once outside the Kingdom but are inside now by the grace of our Savior and King, Jesus. And we should daily remind ourselves what that Kingdom is like. Remind ourselves that we are to lovingly obey the King. Remind ourselves of who is in the Kingdom. And remind ourselves that we are called to live an ethos of the Kingdom, rooted in the command to love God and to love our neighbors as ourselves.

Set the Kingdom before you every day.

Set the King before you every day.

Set the Kingdom ethos before you every day.

Daily grow in passion for the Kingdom of God. Work to have that same passion for the Kingdom that Jesus did here on Earth. More and more, let it become "the center of gravity" and of "supreme importance" in all that you say and do.

In doing so, you will gain a different set of eyes that see things completely differently. Kingdom eyes see a Kingdom that stretches out far beyond this world. You will see a Kingdom teeming with saints and angels living rightly together. You will see justice and peace and kindness and joy and love coming from the Great King. And you will that you are part of it.

As a citizen, you will find happiness and contentment and hope in a completely different way. Your ultimate happiness and hope isn't grounded in the pleasures or people of this life. You will see a King in charge of everything, who loves and blesses His people. You will celebrate the goodness the King gives and submit with trust when He allows trials and suffering to enter your lives. You will understand the words to the song, "It Is Well with My Soul" by Horatio Spafford and Philip Bliss:

When peace like a river, attendeth my way,

When sorrows like sea billows roll

Whatever my lot, thou hast taught me to say

It is well, it is well, with my soul

As a Kingdom citizen, you will understand these words because your purpose, happiness, and hope aren't rooted in the blessings that come your way but in the unchanging, loving, righteous, gentle, and patient King who dispenses the blessings. And because of all this, as a citizen who lays hold of the Kingdom of God, you won't disengage from the world. You won't withdraw. Just the opposite.

Ironically, this invisible Kingdom is meant to be a light on a hill. When we turn away from the counterfeit claims for our minds and hearts and embrace the King and His ethos, it is just that: a bright shining light on hill—the invisible made visible in the lives of believers around the world. In a world too full of hate and mistrust and depression and sadness and emptiness, the Kingdom emerges in the lives of citizens around the world as they love God with all their heart and love their neighbor as themselves. Instead of expats conforming to this world, we become embassies full of life and power and love that shine out. In a world where the darkness is getting darker, in times when everything seems to be falling apart, the bright light of the King, the Kingdom, and its ethos is all the more important to us and to those who are seeking the light.

The Kingdom of God changes everything. It is worth giving everything up for in order to gain it. Just as Jesus taught.

ACKNOWLEDGMENTS

I am indebted to many for this book.

This book had its genesis with the Winers and their wives who entrusted their Sunday mornings to me at our annual beach weekend retreats to preach this material. Thank you Glenn and Donna, Gordon and Jean, Leo and Su, Dave and Diane, Steve and Linda, John and Pam, Tommy and Jeanne, Harry and Sissy.

My Community Group at Redeemer Church of Arlington patiently, graciously, and encouragingly sat through my weekly presentations of near finished material and provided invaluable feedback. Thank you Dale and Gay, Emily, Anthony and Cameron, Wil and Cathy, Carolyn, Ann, Josh and Emily, Hannah and Matthew, Evan and Meagan.

Carolyn McCulley provided excellent and much needed editorial help. She was thorough and insightful, especially with text that needed a lot of help or, in more than one case, removal. Where the book reads well, credit Carolyn. All remaining errors and failures in this book are mine and mine alone.

Katie Martin originally agreed to design the cover for this book. Before attempting any artistic effort, she read the entire manuscript. In the process, she became more than just the designer: she helped bring this book to print. After designing a cover that I am completely and enthusiastically happy with, she assisted in the final production effort that enabled me to self-publish. In retrospect, she was simply the Lord's gracious gift to a foolish old man who had no idea what he was getting himself into when he first decided to self-publish. I am muchly indebted to her.

Made in the USA
Middletown, DE
29 March 2021